HOW TO DESIGN A BOAT

Other titles of interest

Principles of Yacht Design
Lars Larsson & Rolf Eliasson
ISBN 0 7136 3855 9
A comprehensive and up to date textbook covering all aspects of yacht design.

Complete Amateur Boat Building: 4th edition
Michael Verney
ISBN 0 7136 5731 6
The standard source of information for both amateurs and professionals for many years, this new edition now incorporates the many new products that have revolutionised boat building.

This is Boat Interior Construction
M Naujok
ISBN 0 7136 3612 2
This book shows you, step by step, with the help of over 400 colour photographs, exactly how to alter the standard layout of your production boat or completely fit out a hull.

Boat Electrical Systems
Dag Pike
ISBN 0 7136 3451 0
This very practical straightforward guide demystifies the subject for the average owner wishing to fit out a boat, install new electronic equipment or simply sort out an annoying electrical problem.

Boatowner's Mechanical and Electrical Manual
2nd edn
Nigel Calder
ISBN 0 7136 4291 2
This bestselling DIY manual for boatowners has been completely revised and brought up to date.

Spray
Bruce Roberts-Goodson
ISBN 0 7136 4086 3
This book explores the rebuilding of *Spray*, analyses her design, gives highlights of the record setting voyage and recounts the building and sailing experiences of owners of over 800 *Spray* replicas and copies.

You can obtain these books from bookshops and chandlers. In the case of difficulty use the order form at the back of the book.

HOW TO DESIGN
A BOAT
—— John Teale ——

ADLARD COLES NAUTICAL
London

Published 1992 by Adlard Coles Nautical
an imprint of A & C Black (publishers) Ltd
35 Bedford Row, London WC1R 4JH

Copyright © John Teale 1992

First edition 1992
Reprinted 1995

ISBN 0-7136-3529-0

A CIP catalogue record for this book is available
from the British Library.

Typeset in 11/12 pt Century by
J. W. Arrowsmith Ltd, Bristol BS3 2NT

Printed and bound in Great Britain by
J. W. Arrowsmith Ltd, Bristol BS3 2NT

Contents

Contents

1 Preliminary sketches and calculations

Anyone having a reasonable eye for a fair curve and the merest smattering of mathematics can design a boat. The first effort may not be a world beater but, if built, should perform perfectly well and give a good deal of pleasure. What bothers most people having a go for the first time are the basics. How do I know how deep she will float? Where should I put the centreboard? What sort of area should the rudder be? And so on. In this book simple answers will be attempted to such questions while, by the end, the design process should have been taken far enough for the interested reader to be able to look at the published drawings of any type of craft, study them, and then, understanding what has gone on, use them as the basis for a design of their own.

Early on in the design process an approximate weight for the completed craft will need to be known, so some idea of how the boat is to be built will be required. Construction is a vast subject with much written about particular methods which, even so, leave many possibilities unexplored. In Chapter 6 some general structural guidelines are given, but the designer should really have a close look at examples of the type of build that interests him and learn from those. Imagine, while drawing, that you are going to build the vessel yourself and act accordingly.

Equipment

It takes a fair amount of gear to take a design to the stage at which the drawings can be presented to a builder with confidence, but the initial arrangement sketches require only:

- an ordinary clutch pencil with some HB leads and a drum sharpener
- some form of straight edge about 2–3 ft (600–900 mm) long
- a set square (clear plastic) with something like 8 in (200 mm) sides
- a really good pencil rubber
- a sheet of A1 cartridge paper
- a scale rule, either imperial or metric to suit your tastes, incorporating useful scales like $\frac{1}{2}$ in, $\frac{3}{4}$ in and 1 in = 1 ft (or 1 : 25, 1 : 15 and 1 : 10 metrically). It is quite hopeless trying to concoct some ingenious scale as, for instance, $3\frac{1}{2}$ mm = 1 in so as to be able to use a child's school ruler.

The longest French Curve that is available will also be useful occasionally, to harden up freehand sketches, supplemented by a smaller version with tighter curves. A drawing board is not strictly necessary at this stage – any table of convenient height will do. A drawing office supplies shop can provide all the gear mentioned. Additional equipment needed by the more ambitious will be described later.

The initial sketch

Now we'll have a go at drawing the initial sketches of the craft shown in Fig 1. This is a day sailer 20 ft (6 m) in length. Without

2

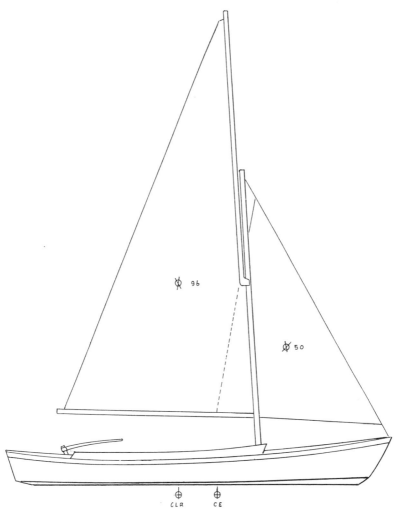

Fig 1   This is the boat that will be used as an example; a 20 ft
(6 m) day sailer.

the rig and with a different layout she could equally well be an
outboard powered vessel or even a motorboat with a low power
inboard engine. The hull form would be the same in all cases.
Don't worry about the meagre drawing tools you possess;

astonishingly accurate curves can be constructed freehand with patience and plentiful use of the rubber.

In what follows:

Loa is length overall, from stem to stern down the centreline not counting excrescences such as bowsprits and bumpkins.
Lwl is length on the waterline.
lwl (lower case first l) is load waterline – the waterline the boat is designed to float at.
Bwl is beam on the waterline.
D is the depth of the bottom of the main hull below the waterline at midships. It is not the same as draught, which is taken to the bottom of the keel at its deepest part.

All these are shown on Fig 2.

Looking at the above-water profile Fig 1, Lwl has turned out to be about 17 ft (5.2 m) because that gave what was considered a pleasing outline on an overall length of 20 ft (6 m).

Freeboard and sheer

Freeboard is the height of the deck edge above the water; typical freeboards at the bow are given in Fig 3. On a 17 ft Lwl, the freeboard at the bow is about 2.2 ft. Fig 2 also shows that freeboard at the stern is freeboard at the bow divided by 1.4, so here the figure would be $2.2 \div 1.4 = 1.6$ ft. The lowest part of the sheer curve occurs about two-thirds the overall length from the bow.

These freeboard recommendations are only guides, and many modern vessels have higher and less curvy deck edges. High freeboard brings unwelcome windage but makes for a marginally drier boat and adds something to stability by delaying the point where the deck edge goes under water. At that moment resistance to further heeling is suddenly reduced. A coaming adds freeboard, and being set back from the deck edge looks less high than topsides carried up to the same height. Reverse

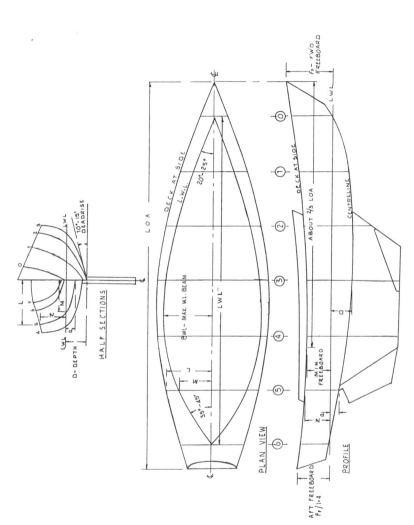

Fig 2 A round bilge version of the day sailer on which various of the terms used (such as Loa and waterline length) are shown.

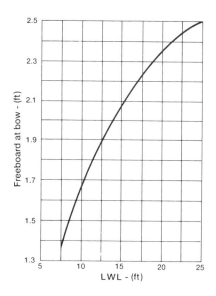

Fig 3   Suggested freeboard at the bow based on waterline length.

and S-shaped sheers can add height where it is needed (to give added hull depth in the way of accommodation, for instance) but are difficult to make attractive visually.

Convention has it that the bow is drawn facing to the right so that the starboard side is seen. This is the side on which the large oar or 'steerboard' was secured in the days before rudders were used. It is still traditionally the most important side of the boat in that starboard cabins and alleyways tend to be allocated to owners and officers.

Incidentally, don't be misled into thinking that a straight line sheer will look classy. It probably won't because, viewed from the side, the centreline of the boat at the bows (and to lesser extent at the stern) is further away from the eyes than is the middle of the vessel. This creates the optical illusion that the ends are drooping downwards. If the sheer is to look straight then some upward sweep of the deck edge is needed, particularly towards the bow.

The above-water profile drawing of Fig 1 can now be completed by adding the area below the lwl, but first we must estimate waterline beam.

Beam

Possible waterline beams (Bwl) based on waterline length are shown in Fig 4. In the example, waterline length (Lwl) is 17 ft (5.2 m) so Bwl is about 5.2 ft (1.6 m). Beam on deck is somewhere between 1.1 and 1.2 times waterline beam, so here maximum beam on deck would be between 5.7 ft (1.7 m) and 6.2 ft (1.9 m).

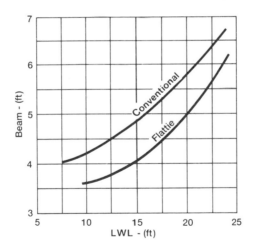

Fig 4 Suggested waterline beam at its maximum point based on waterline length. A flattie is a flat-bottomed boat whose recommended design features are further explored in Chapter 2.

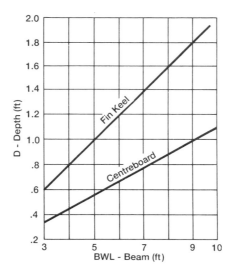

Fig 5   Approximate depth of hull below the waterline at midships for fin keelers and centreboarders. Based on waterline beam.

Depth

Another graph, Fig 5, shows the relationship between waterline beam and the depth of the main hull below the waterline at midships, D (Fig 2). A centreboarder will be a lighter boat than a fin keeler, so for a 5.2 ft waterline beam, a centreboarder's depth would be around 0.57 ft, while that of a fin keeler would be just over 1 ft.

There is another method of estimating depth of the main hull, D. This involves using what is known as the **block coefficient**, C_b. This is the ratio between the actual immersed volume of the hull to the product of waterline length, waterline beam and depth at midships. In other words, the ratio between the actual volume compared with the volume if it had been a box underwater, ie not shaped at all.

So, $C_b = \Delta \times 35/(L \times B \times D)$ where Δ is the weight of the hull in tons (ie its displacement; but don't worry about the term displacement at the moment. It will be explained shortly and for the present can be considered as simply the weight of the boat completely fitted out and carrying its normal complement of crew, fuel, water, stores and so on. The multiplier, 35, converts tons to the equivalent volume in cubic feet of sea water (explanations later). L is waterline length, B is waterline beam and D is depth of hull – everything at midships and measured in feet

What we wanted from this potential calculation was D, so the formula can be re-written as: $D = \Delta \times 35/(L \times B \times C_b)$ and if the weight had been in pounds rather than tons we could put: $D = \Delta(\text{in lb})/(L \times B \times C_b \times 64)$.

What we still don't have is a number for C_b. An approximation (the actual figure will depend, of course, on how fine the underwater lines are) for hard chine forms is that $C_b =$ between 0.34 and 0.36. On round bilge types the figure will be a little lower, say $C_b = 0.32$.

So far we have been considering a 20 ft (6 m) day sailer. We don't know its weight at the moment, but a boatbuilder or friend might be able to estimate hull weight for you or you may be able to assess it yourself: see Chapter 2. To that figure you need to add crew weight, sails, spars, auxiliary, fuel, water and everything else you could carry aboard.

Suppose we chose a centreboard, hard chine version. A builder might estimate, say, 650 lb (292.5 kg) for the hull. To that you might add 400 lb (180 kg) for the other bits and pieces mentioned. The grand total is $650 + 400 = 1050$ lb (472 kg). Put that in the formula. We know L is 17 ft and B is 5.2 ft. $D = \Delta(\text{in lb})/(L \times B \times C_b \times 64)$ or, assuming C_b is 0.34, $D = 1050/(17 \times 5.2 \times 0.34 \times 64)$. That is, $D = 0.55$ ft. From Fig 5 showing D, a figure of 0.57 ft for D was found, so two differing schemes gave much the same result, which is encouraging! These D figures are pretty approximate but one has to start somewhere, and later on the results will be checked.

A fin keeler is presumed to have a ballast ratio of about 33 per cent. That is, if the overall weight including keel was 1800 lb and the fin keel itself weighed 600 lb the ballast ratio would be $600 \div 1800$, or 0.33, which is 33 per cent.

So now we have sufficient ingredients for the first, rough, freehand sketches of the hull to be completed. Overall and waterline lengths are known, as are the figures for waterline and overall beam. The freeboard and sheer line have been decided upon and the depth of the hull below the water estimated.

Fig 6 shows a hard chine, centreboard version of the day sailer in Fig 1. We might as well begin with this hard chine type as being the easiest to design (and build).

First draw a straight line representing the waterline, lwl, in profile, and aim on drawing the sketch about 12 in (300 mm) long. This means suitable scales would be $\frac{1}{2}$ in = 1 ft or 1:25. At an appropriate distance below lwl and exactly parallel to it draw another straight line as the centreline of the plan view. A plan view is the shape of the boat looking down on it from above. Draw in the profile of the deck and then the keel or centreline. The depth of the hull at midships below the waterline is known, D, and on all slow-speed vessels like this one the transom bottom must be above the lwl to allow a smooth flow of water round the stern.

Now draw in the deck line in plan view. Maximum beam has been decided and we can assume on this version that it occurs at midships. At its aft end the deck might end in a transom, as shown, or come to a point and so create a double-ended craft. A double ender is slippery and seaworthy; a transom stern allows more space inside the boat and may permit a little more speed, especially on a reach or run or when under power. Too wide a transom can create problems in following seas when a big wave could lift the very buoyant, wide transom and in so doing force the bows deep into the water. This is the attitude a boat takes immediately before a broach, which is most unpleasant.

Having drawn the deck line in plan (and it should be slightly fuller over its stern half than forward, even with a double ender) divide the waterline length into an even number of equal spaces. In the example six divisions have been used and these are called stations. Since the boat is 17 ft (5.18 m) on the waterline, the

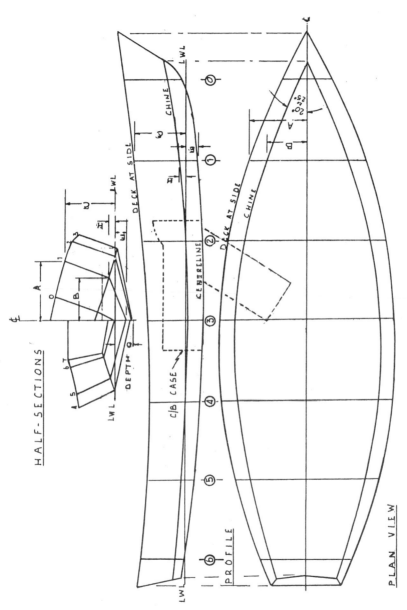

Fig 6   A first lines plan of a hard chine version of the day sailer.

11

stations are $17 \div 6 = 2$ ft 10 in (0.86 m) apart. Make sure the station lines are vertical and parallel to one another.

Next draw a half section at midships. This is a cross section through one side of the hull. The height and beam of the deck are known. From this point draw a line down through the beam on the waterline (also known). Then from the keel or centreline at the depth D and at an angle of between 10° and 15° put in the bottom line. Where this intersects the line down from the deck edge gives the height and width of the chine at midships. This point can be transferred to the profile and plan view outlines. Finally draw in the chine in plan and profile, roughly parallel to the deck and keel lines respectively, before sitting back to admire the result.

Fill in the other half-sections with those from stations 0–3 inclusive to the right of the centreline, and stations 4–6 inclusive to the left. Station 1 is drawn in detail on Fig 6. Dimensions A, B, C, E and H must correspond in all views.

Generally speaking a boat with a steeply vee'd bottom or rise of floor will heel more easily, but will knife along to windward more effectively than a flatter-floored rival. It will float a little deeper too, which helps windward performance, for there is no real substitute for depth of hull in the water to counteract leeway. Big rudders, centreplates and fins all help, of course, but are not the complete answer. Boats with shallower vee bottoms come into their own when reaching or running and under power. The rise of floor must increase as the bottom approaches the bow to reduce slamming in a head sea.

Looking at Fig 6 you may wonder why the shape of the load waterline (lwl) in plan view is not drawn in as it appears to have been with the round bilge version in Fig 2. It could have been, but its presence is not all that helpful on chine boats, and leads to problems in fairing which are best avoided at this stage.

All this probably seems a very mechanical way of drawing one particular type of boat, but there is no reason why this half-decker should not be transformed into a little cruising boat with the addition of a cuddy or what-have-you. It could equally well be a double ender of a totally different length and sheer line without making any difference to the design processes so far described.

As we continue, a system of checks will be used to validate what has been done in the initial stages and allow some freedom to amend. Here is the first of these checks.

We must now find the volume of the underwater area of the boat for reasons that will be explained in Chapter 2 and, at the same time, calculate the position of the fore and aft centre of area of the underwater volume. This centre is known as the lcb (longitudinal centre of buoyancy) and is determined by using multipliers, or levers, as shown in Tables 1 and 2. It's very straightforward.

Displacement calculation

The volume of displacement is found by working out the underwater area (below lwl) of each halfsection and then putting these figures into a table. Volume can then be translated into a weight, which should equal the weight of the boat – but more on this in Chapter 2.

On a hard chine boat areas can be calculated simply by dividing each half-section into rectangles and triangles as appropriate. Remember to measure areas on one side of the centreline only for each section.

The working of the calculation is straightforward and the example in Table 2 refers to the 20-footer. The Simpson Multipliers (SM) start at 1 on station 0 and continue as 4 and then 2 for as long as necessary. They end up as 4 and finally 1 again. Table 1 maps this out for various numbers of stations. The levers start at 0 on the midships station and then work outwards as 1, 2, 3 and so on as far as necessary. Finally the total of the half areas multiplied by Simpson Multipliers is itself multiplied by the common interval (the spacing between the stations) and then by 2/3. Common interval in this case is 2 ft 10 in or 2.83 ft (0.85 m). Although there was no area at station 6, the aft end

Table 1 Layout of the displacement and lcb calculations for typical numbers of stations

Station	Area	SM	Product	Lever	Product
0		1		3	
1		4		2	
2		2		1	_____
3		4			Total
4		2		1	_____
5		4		2	
6		1	_____	3	_____
			Total		Total
			_____		_____

Station	Area	SM	Product	Lever	Product
0		1		4	
1		4		3	
2		2		2	
3		4		1	_____
4		2			Total
5		4		1	_____
6		2		2	
7		4		3	
8		1	_____	4	_____
			Total		Total
			_____		_____

Station	Area	SM	Product	Lever	Product
0		1		5	
1		4		4	
2		2		3	
3		4		2	
4		2		1	_____
5		4			Total
6		2		1	_____
7		4		2	
8		2		3	
9		4		4	
10		1	_____	5	_____
			Total		Total
			_____		_____

Table 2 The displacement and lcb calculation for the hard chine version of the 20-footer when she was still in the freehand sketch stage

Common interval (station spacing) = 2.83 ft

Station	Area sq ft	SM	Product	Lever	Product
0	—	1	—	3	—
1	0.21	4	0.84	2	1.68
2	0.65	2	1.30	1	1.30
					2.98
3	0.84	4	3.36	—	—
4	0.64	2	1.28	1	1.28
5	0.29	4	1.16	2	2.32
6	—	1	—	3	—
			7.94		3.60

Displacement in cu ft = $2/3 \times 7.94 \times 2.83 = 14.98$
Displacement in lb = $14.98 \times 64 = 958$ lb in salt water
Longitudinal centre of buoyancy (lcb) = $\frac{3.6 - 2.98}{7.94} \times 2.83 = 0.22$ ft aft of midships

lcb should be a little way aft of midships, as it is here.

of the waterline length, in the case of a motor boat with an immersed transom there would have been.

The answer so far is in cubic feet. To translate this to a weight multiply by 64, because a cubic foot of sea water weighs 64 lb. If the answer had been in m³, multiply by 1025 for a figure in kg; a cubic metre of sea water weighs 1025 kg. A cubic foot of fresh water weighs 62.5 lb(1000 kg/m³).

Taking the lcb now, the results of multiplying by the levers are totalled – one total for forward of midships and another for aft. The smaller total is subtracted from the larger and this result is multiplied by the distance between the stations (the common interval) and divided by the volume total under the

15

Product column. The lcb should fall between 50 and 55 per cent of the waterline length aft of station 0.

Enough of these mathematical conundrums for the moment. Fuller explanations follow in subsequent chapters and we shall look at the round bilge fin keeler and a flattie version; and some possible areas for rudders, fin keels, centreboards and sails to complete the first sketches.

2 Completing the preliminary designs

In this chapter we shall look at displacement and the longitudinal centres of gravity and buoyancy (lcg and lcb). The initial sketches can then be fleshed out with the addition of the rudder, keel or centreboard, and sails.

Displacement

This is all to do with the Archimedes principle, which states that the weight of a floating body must be equal to the weight of the displaced fluid. In other words, if a boat was lowered gently into a tank brim-full of sea water, the weight of water that flowed over the edge of the tank would be exactly equal to the weight of the boat. The same would apply if the liquid were, say, mercury or petrol or fresh water. Its displaced weight would be the same as the boat's, though of course the *volume* of liquid to equal that weight would be different in each case. Very little mercury would be displaced (it weighs something like 750 lb/cu ft ($12\,075$ kg/m^3) but, by comparison, quite a lot of petrol, which is lighter than sea water, would be displaced. Fresh water is lighter too, so it follows that since a greater volume will be displaced to equal the weight, a boat will float a little deeper in fresh water than in salt.

In the case of the 20-footer, its underwater volume, assuming it floats at the depth we estimated, is 14.98 cu ft (0.42 m^3) (see Table 2 in Chapter 1). Since sea water weighs 64 lb/cu ft (1025 kg/m^3) the weight of the displaced sea water must be $14.98 \times 64 = 958$ lb (434 kg) and that must also be the weight of the boat if it is to float at lwl.

So far, so good? The *real* weight of the boat is still an unknown, though it is hoped that it will be around 958 lb (431 kg) (the displacement to our desired waterline). We must now rectify that omission.

Table 3 gives weights for some typical boatbuilding materials. With the sheet products of steel, aluminium alloy and ply weight is given in lb/sq ft per millimetre of thickness and in kg/m^2 per millimetre of thickness. Thus, 3 mm steel weighs $3 \times 1.6 = 4.8$ lb sq ft (234 kg/m^2) while 9 mm ply comes out at $9 \times 0.137 = 1.23$ lb/sq ft (6.15 kg/m^2).

Table 3   Weights of boatbuilding materials

Material	Weight lb/cu ft (kg/m^3)	Weight lb/mm thick/sq ft (kg/mm thick/m^2)
Cedar	24 (385)	
African mahogany	32 (512)	
Douglas fir	33 (530)	
Larch	35 (560)	
Teak	41 (655)	
Oak (English)	45 (720)	
Cast iron	450 (7200)	
Lead	710 (11 400)	
Steel		1.6 (7.8)
Aluminium alloy		0.56 (2.73)
Plywood		0.137 (0.67)

Table 4 Preliminary weight calculation for a 20 ft day sailer

Item	Ply thickness mm	Weight/sq ft lb	Area sq ft	Weight lb
Bottom	9	1.2	81	97
Sides	9	1.2	64	77
Deck	6	0.83	25	20
Transom	12	1.65	5	8
Centreboard case	12	1.65	12	20
Centreboard	24	3.3	6	19
Rudder	24	3.3	5	17
Bulkheads	6	0.83	10	8
Total				266
Add two thirds				177
Total				443
Spars and sails				55
Coamings and floorboards				40
Thwarts and seats				25
Fittings				10
Crew				300
Grand total				873

The weight calculation for the 20-footer is shown in Table
4. All the ply structures are given an estimated area and thus
weight. These are then totalled and in this case they come to
266 lb. Two thirds of that is then added in to allow for items
of solid timber, such as chines, gunwales, keel, stringers, structural floors, frames and so on. So, 266 lb plus 177 lb is 433 lb,
which represents the estimated weight of the bare hull. Add to
this fitting-out and crew weights and we have a grand total of
873 lb.

This is near enough our hoped for 958 lb for work to proceed
with some confidence. After all, there are still some weights we
could add – what about an outboard plus fuel; an anchor and
warp; and even a picnic basket? And the lines plan is still in its
infancy, really. The boat may float a little high in the water at
worst. If the numbers were wildly apart, however, measures

would have to be taken to increase or decrease displacement as appropriate. Beam could, for instance, be increased or decreased; the keel line lifted or dropped; the chine line altered. None of these activities would have very much effect on structural weight but, done boldly, they could dramatically alter the displacement.

In this example two thirds of the sheet material weight was added to allow for the solid timber structure. Two thirds is an arbitrary but quite reasonable figure for conventional hard chine construction. However, with modern, lightweight structural methods where epoxy/glass connections are widely used and chines and gunwales may be of resin/glass lay-ups rather than solid timber, the figure of two thirds may be changed to one third. The latter is also appropriate when dealing with steel, aluminium alloy and even glassfibre, where the surface areas of hull, bulkheads and so forth are used as the basis.

On the other hand, in a really heavily framed chine boat, the solid timber may well weigh at least as much as the ply. Table 5 demonstrates this for a 14 ft 6 in by 6 ft 9 in (4.4 m × 2 m) cruising dinghy (Figs 7, 8 and 9). At the end, 10 per cent has been added to the grand total to allow for t.e many things that will have been forgotten!

Fig 8 shows a structural section for the boat which, incidentally, has a double bottom that drains into the rudder trunk. The crew sit on battened seats inside the vessel. Centreboard and rudder are not included on the timber list, since they are of GRP.

So, if in doubt about the weight ratio between sheet material and solid, do a rough calculation to set your mind at rest. With traditional timber construction always add up individual items and do not rely on ratios.

Table 6 shows the displacement calculation for the 14 ft 6 in (4.35 m) cruising dinghy in Fig 7. Displacement comes to 850 lb (382 kg), which compares quite well with the weight total of 603 lb (271 kg) before fitting out. As a matter of interest the block coefficient has been worked out – do you remember that from Chapter 1? Here it is 0.36, which falls in line with the predicted figure of between 0.34 and 0.36.

Table 5 Preliminary weight calculations for a 14 ft 6 in dinghy

Item	Scantling	Wt per ft or sq ft	Area sq ft	Weight lb
Ply				
Foredeck	6 mm	0.825 lb	6	5
Hull sides	6 mm	0.825	60	50
Hull bottom	6 mm	0.825	82	68
D'ble bottom	9 mm	1.24	66	83
Transom	9 mm	1.24	3	4
Centreboard case	9 mm	1.24	14	17
Rudder trunk	9 mm	1.24	4	5
Floors	9 mm	1.24	14	18
				250 lb
Longitudinals	*Inches*		*ft run*	
	$2\frac{1}{2} \times 1\frac{1}{4}$	0.73	126	92
	$1\frac{1}{4} \times 1$	0.30	36	11
	9×1	2.12	28	60
	4×1	0.94	28	26
	$4\frac{1}{2} \times 2$	2.12	17	36
				225 lb
Transverses	$2\frac{1}{2} \times 1\frac{1}{4}$	0.73	100	73 lb

Grand total = 250 + 225 + 73
= 548
Plus 10% = 603 lb

It was also suggested in Chapter 1 that the lcb be sited between 50 and 55 per cent of the waterline length aft of station 0. Here it is 55 per cent so all is well.

We have more calculations to do, however.

Longitudinal centre of gravity (lcg) and longitudinal centre of buoyancy (lcb)

Going back to the concept of the tankful of water in which a boat floats, suppose the water was frozen and the vessel lifted

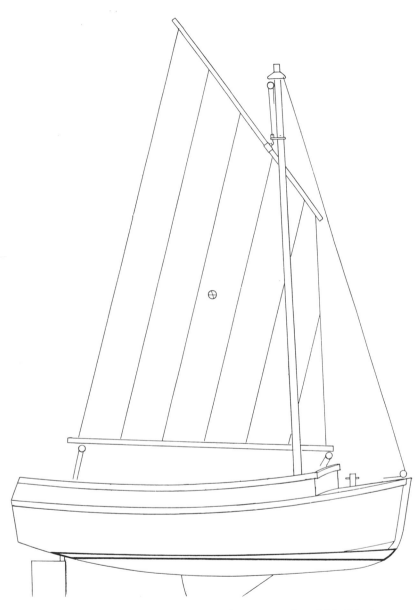

Fig 7   A balanced lug cruising dinghy measuring 14 ft 6 in by 6 ft 9 in (4.4 m by 2 m) with sail area 80 sq ft (7.4 m²). The rudder ships down through a trunk and the transom is cut away for a long shaft outboard.

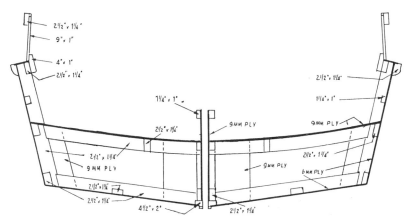

Fig 8   A scantling section through the cruising dinghy and used for the preliminary weight estimate.

out. There would now be a depression in the ice corresponding to the underwater shape of the boat. This must have a centre of area. After all, if the depression was used as a mould, and concrete was poured in and then lifted out after setting, it would have a balancing point. This point is known as the longitudinal centre of buoyancy (**lcb**) and the boat pivots about it in the water. The position of the lcb was calculated for the 20-footer in Table 2; it turned out to be 0.22 ft aft of midships. The underwater shape also has a vertical centre of area known as the vertical centre of buoyancy (**vcb**) at some distance below the waterline, but that is of no concern at the moment.

The longitudinal centre of all the weights connected with the boat (if the hull were balanced out of the water it would pivot about this point which is known as the longitudinal centre of gravity (**lcg**)) must now be found. For this we continue to use the recently completed weights calculation in Table 4. Table 7 sets out the calculations. For each of the weights previously used, a longitudinal centre of area or gravity position is estimated and written down as shown. Weights and their distance forward or aft of midships are then multiplied. The various figures are

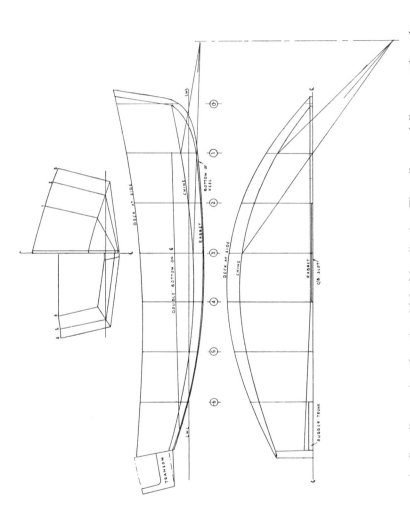

Fig 9 The rough, first lines plan for the 14 ft 6 in dinghy. The diagonal lines cutting through the forebody are generator lines for the conic projection and will be explained in Chapter 3.

Table 6 Displacement calculations for a 14 ft 6 in dinghy

Frame or station	Area sq ft	SM	Product	Lever	Product
0	—	1	—	3	—
1	0.14	4	0.56	2	1.12
2	0.58	2	1.16	1	1.16
3	1.06	4	4.24		2.28
4	1.10	2	2.20	1	2.20
5	0.45	4	1.80	2	3.60
6	—	1	—	3	—
			9.96		5.80

Displacement to Lwl. Frames at 2 ft centres
Scale 1 in = 1 ft

Displacement $= \frac{2}{3} \times 9.96$ ft $\times 2 \times 64$
$\qquad = 850$ lb

Block coefficient $(C_b) = \frac{850}{12 \times 5.75 \times 0.54 \times 64}$
$\qquad = 0.36$

Longitudinal centre of buoyancy (lcb) $= \frac{(5.8-2.28)}{9.96} \times 2$
$\qquad = 0.7$ ft aft station 3

If lcb is 0.7 ft aft of station 3, it is 6.7 ft aft of station 0 (stations are at 2 ft centres). Thus the lcb is:

lcb $= \frac{6.7}{12} \times 100$
$\qquad = 55$ per cent of waterline length aft of station 0
$\qquad$ (waterline length is 12 ft)

totalled; a spot of subtraction and division follows; and soon enough, an lcg figure appears. This turns out to be 0.6 ft aft of midships.

The distance between the lcb (Table 2) and lcg (Table 7) positions is small (0.38 ft) and not worth bothering about, although the consequences of a wide gap between the two centres is shown in Fig 10. The boat will trim until the new lcb (new, because trimming has altered the underwater hull shape) is in line with the lcg.

On a boat like this one where crew weight is a significant and movable factor, and where unthought-of items creep aboard

Table 7 Calculation for lcg on a 20 ft day sailer

Item	Weight lb	Lcg from midships ft Forward	Aft	Moment lb ft Fwd	Aft
Bottom	97	—	—	—	—
Sides	77	—	—	—	—
Deck	20	2.0		40	
Transom	8		9.25		74
Centreboard case	20	1.25		25	
Centreboard	19	1.25		24	
Rudder	17		10.00		170
Bulkheads	8		1.5		12
Totals	266			89	256

Lcg so far is $\frac{256-89}{266} = 0.65$ ft aft of midships
Use this information for the next item

Item	Weight lb	Forward	Aft	Fwd	Aft
Two thirds ply hull	177		0.65		115
Sails and spars	55	3.25		179	
Coamings, floorboards	40		1.0		40
Thwarts, seats	25		4.0		100
Fittings	10	—	—	—	—
Crew	300		1.1		300
Grand total	873			268	811

Final lcg is $\frac{811-268}{873} = 0.6$ ft aft midships

Where a dash occurs in the lcg or Moments columns it has been assumed that the lcg is at midships. (A **moment** is a weight × a distance.)

to be stowed randomly, a limited amount of trim adjustment can be made when the boat is afloat. However, to achieve a level trim with only the weights considered, either some weight will have to be added forward or the hull lines fined forward and filled aft to bring the lcb aft and under the lcg. This could probably be most easily achieved by lowering the chine line towards the stern while lifting it forward. After such alterations, check that the displacement is still what is required and that all fore and aft lines are still sweet and fair.

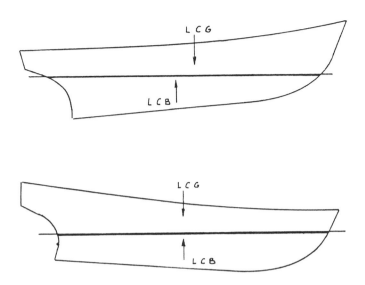

Fig 10   If the lcb and lcg are not in line the boat will trim until they are.

In practice the lcg of the bare hull nearly always ends up near midships and it is with the fitting-out items that adjustments are made. Thus, moving an engine and/or its batteries can alter the lcg quite a bit. Maybe anchor chain can be stowed somewhere other than in a chain locker right forward. Gas bottles can perhaps be sited where they can usefully contribute to the balancing act. As a last resort a small amount of inside ballast could do the trick. Whatever the temptation, do not use items like fuel and water to help sort out a recalcitrant lcg. These should be sited as near the lcb as possible, so that their constantly altering weight does not play too much havoc with the trim. In the lcg calculation their tank weight in half-full condition should be included, and the sums for moments done as with all the other items.

That more or less concludes the calculation side of things, at least as far as the preliminary drawings are concerned.

Other tonnages

Various other tonnages, Registered, Thames and Deadweight, are used when describing ships and (often incorrectly) yachts.

Registered tonnage is the figure that is carved into the main beam of a yacht or otherwise permanently and prominently displayed. Despite the name, it is not a weight at all but an assessment made by the DoT (or someone acting on their behalf as is often the case with yachts) of the internal volume of the vessel. If the volume is in cu ft it is divided by 100 and called tons. If in m^3 it is divided by 2.83 to arrive at the same answer.

When measuring for volume there are certain exempted spaces, such as double bottoms to carry water ballast, which are not measured. This first answer is called the gross tonnage, and from it may be deducted areas such as engine and chart rooms, crew's quarters, and so forth to give register or net tonnage.

The word 'tons' used in this context may derive from the fact that cargo vessels were once assessed on the numbers of casks or 'tuns' of wine they could carry. Harbour dues are traditionally paid on net tonnage, while passenger ship tonnages in promotion blurbs are normally gross. The 50 000 ton *Extravaganza* implies that she is 50 000 tons gross.

Cargo ships, bulk carriers, tankers and the like are usually quoted as being so many tons deadweight (dwt). Deadweight is the weight in tons that a ship can carry when loaded to the maximum permissible draught. Deadweight includes not only cargo but also movable stores, such as provisions, fuel and fresh water. What a ship weighs when completely empty is termed Lightship and therefore Lightship + Deadweight = Load displacement.

Thames Measurement (TM) or Thames Tonnage is:

$$TM = \frac{(L - B) \times B \times \frac{1}{2}B}{94}$$

where L = length and B = beam or, more simply:

$$TM = \frac{(L - B) \times B^2}{188}$$

Until the 1850s this was the tonnage measurement for cargo ships and also the rating measurement for yacht racing. In that form and several minor variations it continued for many years after merchant vessels had adopted a more sensible measurement. Indeed it was often used when describing yachts right up until the Second World War, though not then as a racing rating.

Its drawback is clear. Beam is heavily penalised while the depth of hull and sail area are ignored. Consequently racing yachts were built with ludicrously narrow hulls and, to compensate for the inevitable loss of stability and sail-carrying ability, great draught and enormously heavy ballast keels. These were the notorious British 'plank-on-edge' yachts described by the great Scottish designer G L Watson as approaching Euclid's definition of a line as having length but no breadth. An Essex agricultural implement maker, E H Bentall, designed and built the phenomenally successful 110 ft (33.5 m) yawl *Jullanar* with a length/beam ratio of 6 : 1 (today's figure would be more like 4 : 1) and then proceeded to build a 10-tonner (TM) called *Evolution*, shown in Fig 11. On a waterline length of 50.75 ft (15.2 m) her beam was 6.5 ft (2 m), a length/beam ratio

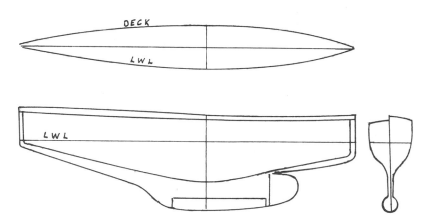

Fig 11   Lines of *Evolution*, an extreme example of the plank-on-edge type of British yacht of the late 1800s. She was actually built in 1880.

of 7.8. Though she was not a success, having stability problems, it shows how far people were prepared to go to fit in with the rating rules of the day.

Hull form

So far we have concentrated on the hard chine version of the day sailer but there are two variants: the flattie shown in Fig 12 and the round bilge version in Fig 13 which first appeared as Fig 2.

Water pushed aside by a boat as it moves through the water is forced downwards as well as sideways. As a consequence its average direction of flow is diagonally downwards and from bow to stern. Water, disturbed from a free run by angles (such as the chines), eddies and becomes turbulent, absorbing power in doing so. Thus the gentler the curves it has to flow along the happier it will be, with the consequence that a round bottom hull will be slightly easier to drive through the water than a chine rival, especially at the velocities at which sailing craft and low speed motor boats commonly travel.

As knots increase the hard chine or vee bottom hull starts to come into its own. Then the water rushing along the bottom and bearing on a surface slightly angled down into its flow (nearly all boats trim by the stern as speeds rise) will have a lift component. That is, it will try to lift the stern, reducing the area of hull in the water and thus the power requirement to drive it. The water will lift a flattish surface more easily than a curved one round which the water will tend to flow rather than push. So a chine form is good for high planing speeds on a sailing vessel and most of the time on a motor boat. It is seaworthy, easier to build than round bottom and unjustly mocked by those who are convinced by the arguments of GRP boatbuilders (glassfibre needs plenty of built-in curves to overcome its inherent floppiness).

There is, of course, more to hull form than simply deciding between chine and round bilge configurations and then aiming for a smooth flow of water round the hull by drawing fair lines. There is, for instance, a matter of how the displacement is to be spread through the length. In other words, should a lot of the underwater volume be concentrated around the middle of the vessel leading to fine, low volume ends, or would full sections towards bow and stern be preferable? The answer is that it mostly depends on the projected speed of the boat. Chapter 5 deals with the subject in more detail, but in the meantime if lines plans shown in this book are used as examples, all should be well. Select the lines of craft which are to perform similar tasks to the one you are sketching.

Power, whether provided by sails or an engine, is used up by making waves as the boat pushes through the water, and in overcoming the friction between hull and water. Methods of reducing the first loss are covered in Chapter 5 dealing with the distribution of displacement. Frictional losses are reduced by cutting down on the area of hull in contact with the water. Hence a fin keel will cause less frictional resistance than a full length keel, and a centreboard, when raised, will create less resistance than either. Thus, if speed is of the essence on, say, a sailing yacht, a fin keel is probably the right choice, though the craft will probably be less steady on the helm than a long-keeler and so may not make quite such a good cruising yacht.

A centreboard, though splendid in reducing wetted area, is difficult to combine with effective (and thus low slung) outside ballast. It can be operated with its slot set in a shallow ballast keel, but the presence of the keel means that some of the potential low wetted area advantages of the centreboard are lost. A bulb of lead or iron may be incorporated at the bottom of the board so that it acts low down when lowered and nestles in a recess formed in the hull in the 'up' position. The board, in such a case, normally operates by sliding vertically down the case, like a dagger board, rather than pivoting. This is an effective scheme, usually called a lifting keel, but the lifting arrangements

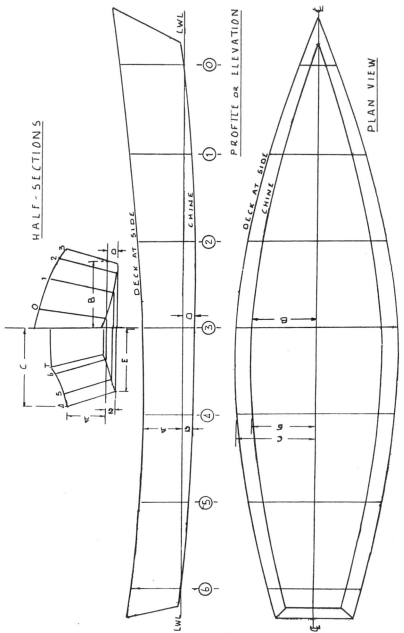

Fig 12   A flat-bottomed version of the day sailer.

tend to be rather costly and complicated, while the whole thing may not be as structurally sound as a true, integral ballast keel.

Let us return to the task of settling on a hull form.

Flatties

These have flat rather than vee bottoms. They should be long, lean, light and low for best results. Recommended waterline beam was shown in Fig 4, and freeboard should not exceed the suggestions made. Given those features a flattie should be a considerable success in calm waters. Of course this type can and has been used on ocean crossings, but generally the inherently more seakindly chine or round bilge types would be preferable. There is little hull in the water (the depth D can be taken as about 1/10th maximum waterline beam) so rudders and centre-plates should be oversize.

Round bilges

Fig 13 shows the 20 ft (6 m) day sailer in round bilge form. First draw the deck/sheerline and the keel/centreline in profile using the suggested depth (D) measurement for a 5.2 ft (1.5 m) waterline beam fin keeler (just over 1 ft (300 mm)) as in Fig 5. Next draw the waterline (lwl) and deck line in plan view. The maximum waterline beam normally occurs a little way aft of midships, as shown. The curve should be somewhat fuller aft than forward. Then sketch in the sections, preferably starting with those occurring at stations 1, 3 and 5. When you are satisfied with those, draw in the remainder. Dimensions L, M, N and P, shown on the half-section at station 5, must correspond in all views with similar rules applying to the remainder of the half-sections.

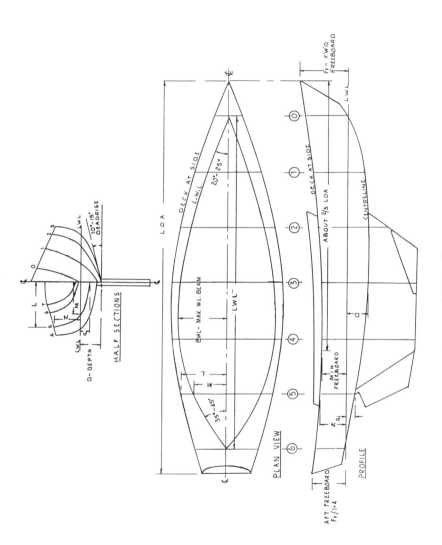

Fig 13   The basic lines plan in round bilge form.

If the sections are barrel-shaped the boat will tend to roll like a barrel so make them straightish over a portion of their underwater area.

Fin keels

From Fig 14 it looks as if the possible area of fin keel for a boat 17 ft on the waterline might be about 17 sq ft (1.6 m^2). This is a fairly large affair, as can be seen, and is not to be confused with the minimum-area keels as used on Flying Fifteens, for instance. Which only goes to show that there are no hard and fast rules! Draw in what pleases you and keep the lower, forward tip of the keel just aft of the mast centreline.

Whatever the shape and area of a fin keel, eventually its longitudinal centre of gravity (lcg) will need to be determined so that the lcg of the boat as a whole lies in the same line as the lcb. Taking the round bilge 20 footer as an example, a quick estimate of the displacement from the half-sections suggested that it was about 1500 lb (675 kg) with the lcb 0.22 ft aft of midships. Previously the weight of the centreboard chine version had been calculated as 873 lb (393 kg). On a fin keel round bilge

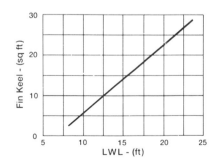

Fig 14   Suggested area of fin keel based on waterline length.

version scantlings would probably be beefed up somewhat. There would, for instance, need to be heavier structural floors to carry the keel bolts and the hull thickness might well be increased to 12 mm. Anyway, assume that weight, without fin, increases by 150 lb from 873 to 1023 lb (460 kg), but that the lcg stays at its original positioning, 0.6 ft aft of midships.

For the juggling we are about to do it will be easiest if distances are measured from station 0. Thus the lcg location of the hull 0.6 ft aft of midships is 3 × 2 ft 10 in (the station spacing) plus 0.6 ft aft of station 0. That is 8.5 + 0.6 = 9.1 ft.

The lcb of the fin keeler is 0.22 ft aft of midships or 8.72 ft aft of station 0. Total weight required is around 1500 lb (675 kg), so if the boat is 1023 lb then the fin, including ballast, must weigh 1500 − 1023 = 477 lb (214 kg) (ballast ratio, 32 per cent).

Fig 15 shows the calculation for the lcg of the fin keel, with the result that its lcg should be 7.9 ft aft of station 0.

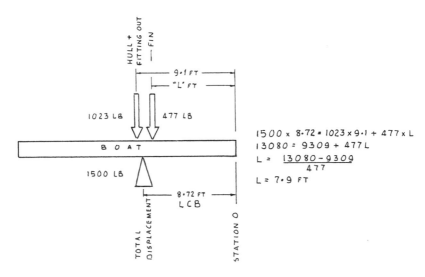

Fig 15 Working out the required position of fin keel and ballast.

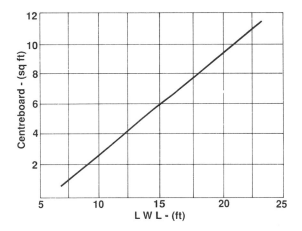

Fig 16   Centreboard area using waterline length as a guide.

Centreboards

Suggested areas are given in Fig 16 based on waterline length. Here waterline length is 17 ft, so the plate area would be about 7.3 sq ft ($0.68 \, \text{m}^2$). The bottom, forward tip of the centreboard when lowered should be a little aft of the mast centreline.

Rudders

Fig 17 shows suggested areas based on lateral plane area. The latter is the area of the underwater profile view; in this case about 29 sq ft ($2.7 \, \text{m}^2$). Rudder area would therefore be about 3.2 sq ft ($0.3 \, \text{m}^2$).

Completing the preliminary designs

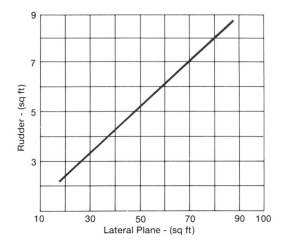

Fig 17   Rudder area based on lateral plane area. The latter is the underwater profile area of the vessel.

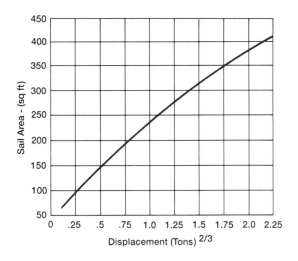

Fig 18   Sail area based on displacement tons.

Sail area

Fig 18 explains these calculations. Sail areas are based on displacement in tons raised to the power of 2/3. This means that the figure for displacement in tons is first squared and then the cube root of that number found. If the displacement of the fin keeler is 1500 lb, that is $1500 \div 2240 = 0.67$ tons. Square 0.67 and the answer is 0.45; the cube root of that is 0.77 and so the sail area would be about 180 sq ft. For the centreboard version of 873 lb (0.39 tons) desirable sail area appears to be about 150 sq ft.

As to distribution of area, on sloop rigs the mainsail commonly has about twice the area of the jib, while on cutters the combined areas of the two headsails tend to be about 70 per cent of that of the main. Thus, on a total area of 180 sq ft the headsails would have a combined area of 75 sq ft and the main, 105 sq ft.

The initial sketches of the boat have now been taken as far as they can. Estimates have been checked and all is now ready for the task of drawing plans accurately. This will take more equipment than has been used so far and in the next chapter suggestions will be made in that direction. Proper lines plans of the day sailer in hard chine and round bilge forms with faired-in keel versions will be shown.

3 Making the working drawings

So far the dreamed-of boat has been sketched in some detail, but only freehand, and though these drawings would form the basis of a design, they are not enough to present to a boatbuilder – unless he happened to be knowledgeable, imaginative, courageous and possibly in need of work. To convert these sketches into useful plans will require quite a bit more drawing gear. But we will assume that the diligent reader will want to soldier on, so here goes.

Drawing board

Though it would be possible to complete the drawings on sheets of paper laid on the dining room table, that would be a tedious undertaking. To make the job bearable a proper drawing board with a parallel motion system, or something similar, is almost a necessity. Such things can be had with simple stands allowing them to be used flat on a table. Upright, engineer's boards and stands are not much use in boat work. The minimum, useful size for a board is A1 and drawing paper can be stuck to it with masking or draughting tape.

Splines

For drawing long curves, flexible plastic battens are used, called splines. These are about 4 ft (1.2 m) in length. They can be had parallel-sided or tapered. The latter are useful since a tighter curve can be drawn with the thinner end than with a normal, parallel-sided spline. So if money is no object one of each is ideal. Battens can also be home-hewn from Perspex. Using 2 mm Perspex sheet, cut a smoothly finished strip about $\frac{1}{4}$ in (6 mm) wide. Splines can be used flat or on edge.

Weights

To hold the battens in place lead weights are used (Fig 19). They weigh about 4 lb (1.8 kg) each and six are plenty. The

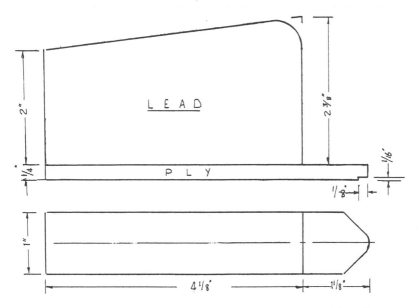

Fig 19   A typical lead weight used in conjunction with splines.

notched plywood base holds the spline down. Weights can be bought complete or made at home by those with casting skills. Home-made ones need painting before use or fingers will rapidly become filthy.

Curves

In some places, such as the sections of a round bottom boat (and below the chine in some hard chine forms), the forward part of buttocks, and the aft length of some waterlines, the curve may be too hard for a spline. In these areas, then, what are known as ship's curves are used. These are of clear plastic and vary in shape from very gentle curves to quite steep ones. Unhappily they are often sold in boxes of 20 or 40 and most of them will be quite useless for yacht work. If it can be arranged, buy two small curves very rounded at one end; one big ramshorn (its shape is as implied); and a couple of long curves which start out gently but finish in bold sweeps (Fig 20).

Fig 20   Five useful ship's curves. The longest are about 2 ft (0.6 m) in length.

Planimeter

This is for measuring area and is used mainly on displacement calculations. Planimeters can be had with variable or fixed scales. The latter are less expensive but still by no means cheap. Fixed scale answers can be converted into the answer in any other scale. If a planimeter measured only in a 1 in scale and the drawing had been done to a $\frac{3}{4}$ in scale, multiply the 1 in scale answer by the square of the inverted actual scale. That is, in the case of a $\frac{3}{4}$ in scale by $4^2/3^2$ or 16/9. If the used scale had been 1/2 in the multiplier would have been 4/1, and so on.

If in doubt, draw a shape of known area (perhaps a square or circle) to the scale you are working on; go round it with the planimeter and find out what the multiplier should be for it to give the right answer. Measure the area two or three times just as a check.

As remarked, planimeters are expensive (though it is possible to pick them up second-hand) and the first and perhaps only-time designer might prefer the infinitely cheaper expedient of using squared transparent paper. This can be had in a variety of scales, both imperial and metric. The idea is to lay the paper over the area to be measured and then count the squares. Make sure this transparent paper can be had in the scale you will need before starting drawing. If not, change the scale! It's a tedious job, though accurate enough for practical purposes.

Of course areas can be divided into rectangles and triangles and then calculated, but squared paper will be quicker and probably more accurate.

Sundries

Though most drawing work will still be done with HB leads, harder H leads may also be handy on occasion. For the grid of a lines plan (of which more in due course) fine ink lines are preferable and are achieved with a cartridge pen, such as the

0.25 Rotring. Pencil drawings do not reproduce very well by the normal dyeline process and need to be inked in, or traced in ink. For this work a thicker pen, such as an 0.4 Rotring, will complement the 0.25.

Sometimes circles or bits of circles need to be drawn. A pair of pencil and ink bows are then necessary, plus, maybe, pencil and ink compasses.

For erasing ink blots and runs (and in all probability there will be some) you can use a sharp scalpel, but you will need to go over the scraped part with a rubber to smooth the surface before having another go with ink.

Now the gear is assembled it is time to start drawing again, starting with a proper lines plan. The freehand sketch already completed is used as a reference. The new lines plan should be drawn to a scale so that it ends up roughly 30 in (0.76 m) long. Much bigger than that and it will be difficult to see everything from bow to stern in one glance and anyway it may not fit on the drawing board. Much smaller and it will be hard to achieve sufficient accuracy.

Just before getting down to detail there is one matter that should be discussed.

Rabbet (or rebate) line

On the rough lines plans so far drawn everything came to a point on the centreline: deck, stem, keel, the lot. But when you consider actual constructional arrangements this can't always be right. On a steel or alloy vessel, the sides and bottom at the centreline are likely to be connected via a stem/keel bar. Since, on a boat of our size, that bar would probably be only 3/8 in(9 mm) thick and its half-breadth to each side of the centreline only 3/16 in (4.5 mm) it is probably accurate enough to assume all endings are on the centreline. But on a GRP boat, for instance, space would have to be made for laminators to lay glass and resin on the inner faces of stem and keel. They couldn't do this properly, especially at the stem, if everything came to a point. So the forward and keel endings would have to have a radius on the centreline.

In the case of a timber-built craft the planking has to be fastened into solid wood at stem and keel and this must be stout enough to accept fastenings and allow an adequate landing between planking and stem or keel. This landing is known as faying surface, and its breadth should be at least twice the thickness of the planking. On ply construction the faying surface should be even broader than that.

The designer sketches out stem and forefoot planking endings to decide on a suitable rabbet line width (Fig 21). Lines plans are usually drawn to the outside of planking and so the width of the rabbet line governs the half-breadth of all endings on the centreline.

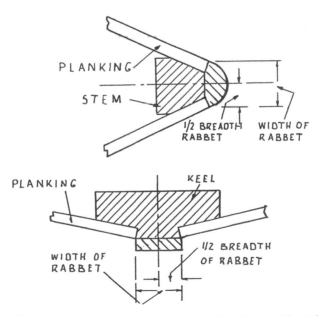

Fig 21 The rabbet line and its width and half-breadth at keel and stem.

At the keel, other considerations also apply. On this day sailer there is either a fin keel or a centreboard and centreboard case. The keel member must be wide enough to accept these and this governs the width of the rabbet line in that area (see Fig 21 again). On this 20-footer the rabbet width might be 5 in (125 mm) in the area of the keel or centreboard, tapering to $2\frac{1}{2}$ in (65 mm) at stem and stern. Half-breadths seen on the lines plan would be half those figures, of course. The rabbet line should be straight in profile where a fin is to be bolted on.

On steel and alloy craft a box fin keel would normally be used welded to the completed shell, so keel rabbet line widths would not apply. On a GRP boat, the fin keel might well be faired into and be integral with the shell to give a shape rather similar to that shown on the round bilge lines plan which follows. Alternatively, the fin could be a heavy metal plate bolted on to the shell.

Canoe stern, round bilge version

Just to show another possibility, Fig 22 demonstrates a canoe stern variant of the half-decker with the fin keel integral with the hull. To ring the changes further, construction is assumed to be traditional wood, not ply, with steamed timbers and mahogany carvel planking. This sort of thing usually turns out to be at least twice as heavy as ply building, with obvious consequences on the depth of the hull below the waterline at midships, D.

It would therefore be advisable to have a go at another weight calculation and Table 8 shows the way. The result appears to be that the hull weight has risen from 443 lb (200 kg) for the ply, centreboard type, Table 4, to a formidable 953 lb (440 kg) for this version and the overall displacement from 785 lb (356 kg) to 1853 lb (840 kg). The weight calculation should be extended to take in fore and aft centres of gravity and moments, as it did in Chapter 2, to produce an LCG position.

Canoe stern, round bilge version

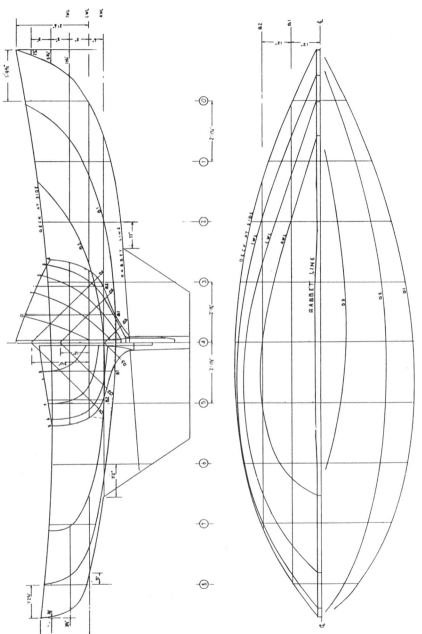

Fig 22 The round bilge, canoe stern version of the day sailer.

47

Table 8 Weight calculations for a 20 ft day sailer in round bilge and traditional timber construction form

Item	Material	Scantling	Wt/sq. ft or ft run	Length or area	Weight lb
Shell	Mahog	5/8 in	1.66 lb	150 sq ft	250
Deck	Mahog	5/8 in	1.66 lb	25 sq ft	42
Rudder	Mahog	3/4 in	1.95 lb	9 sq ft	17
Fin keel	Mahog	5 in	13.3 lb	17 sq ft	226
Timbers	E Oak	$1\frac{1}{4} \times 1$ in	0.4 lb	140 ft	56
Stem	E Oak	3×3 in	2.8 lb	10 ft	28
Keel	E Oak	$7 \times 2\frac{1}{2}$ in	5.46 lb	8 ft	44
Stern post	E Oak	3×3 in	2.8 lb	10 ft	28
Floors	E Oak	2×2 in	1.25 lb	8 ft	10
Deck beams	E Oak	$1\frac{1}{4} \times 1\frac{1}{4}$ in	0.5 lb	18 ft	9
Knees	E Oak				45
Beam shelf	Or pine	$3 \times 1\frac{1}{2}$ in	1.03 lb	42 ft	43
Stringer	Or pine	$2\frac{1}{2} \times 1\frac{1}{2}$ in	0.95 lb	33 ft	28
Bulkheads	Ply	$\frac{1}{2}$ in	1.5 lb	10 sq ft	15
Angle floors	Steel	$30 \times 30 \times 3$	1.0 lb	25 ft	25

					866
				+10%	87
				Hull weight in lb =	953
			+Fitting out and crew weight		450
					1403
			+Ballast keel at, say,		450
			Displacement in lb =		1853

A glance at this weight calculation will show that after the first total of 866 lb, 10 per cent was added. This was to allow for fastening, paint and things that had been forgotten: The item 'knees' was left pretty vague and the figure of 45 lb is simply a guess at a total for stem and stern knees, hanging and lodging knees, a couple of breasthooks and so forth. The construction plan hasn't been drawn at this stage so everything is pretty much guesswork.

Back to the depth of hull below water at midships. This, in Chapter 1, was estimated at a little over 1 ft (300 mm) for a fin keeler of modern construction. Now, in the light of that latest weight calculation, we had better increase that figure somewhat, guessing it to be 1 ft 4 in (400 mm), taken from lwl to the rabbet line at midships. Bearing that figure in mind, elbows can be squared and work on a new, bigger lines plan contemplated. The first, freehand round bilge lines plan can be modified to take in the new D figure, the canoe stern and the reverse tuck to the garboards.

Grid

The basis for all lines plan is an accurate grid which shows waterlines, buttocks (in their straight line views), centrelines, stations and the slope of the diagonals. This grid is usually drawn in ink on cartridge paper which doesn't expand and contract as much as tracing paper. Depending on the size of the drawing board a suitable scale for this 20-footer might be 1 in = 1 ft (1 : 12) or, more accurately, $1\frac{1}{2}$ in = 1 ft (1 : 8). On a metric scale 1 : 10 would seem a good compromise. Nine stations would suffice here with stations 0 and 8 at the ends of lwl. When drawing a grid, be super-accurate. Measure and re-measure. Make sure that lines are really parallel or at right angles, as appropriate.

Waterlines

These are horizontal slices through the hull, parallel to the waterline (lwl) at which it is hoped the boat will float. A waterline appears as a straight line in profile and in section and as a curve in plan. Half-breadths from centreline must agree in sectional and plan views. Three waterlines are drawn here: lwl, Lwl and Awl.

Buttocks

These are vertical slices through the hull parallel to the centre-line. They show up as straight lines on plan and sectional views and as curves in profile. They are marked B1 and B2 in Fig 22. A buttock's height above or below lwl must be the same on profile and sectional views and the point where a buttock cuts a waterline must be on the same vertical line in profile and plan views. Fig 23 shows this.

Diagonals

When drawing the sections on a plan of a round bilge boat it will become apparent that parts of their shape are not very well defined by either waterlines or buttocks. Here diagonals are used to give extra help. They should be arranged so that they cut as many sections at as near right angles as possible. Those shown in Figs 22 and 23 are set at 45 deg to the vertical centreline but there is nothing special about that angle – it simply happened to suit here. Diagonals need not be parallel to each other, though they often are set out that way. Their endings at bow and stern are shown in Fig 23 as is the way they are measured – down their slope from the vertical centreline. Those measurements are generally set out on the plan view. As always, ensure that a nice, fair curve can be drawn through the spots. Define the slope and positioning of the diagonals in the sectional view on the lines plan.

Drawing the lines

The freehand lines plan sketches, already done, will serve as a guide in the initial stages. The deck and rabbet in profile and

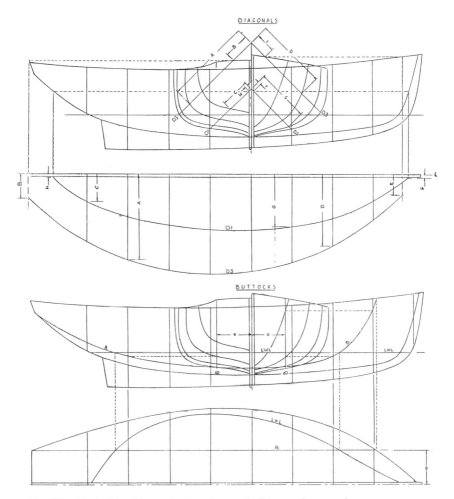

Fig 23 Details of how buttocks and diagonals are drawn
on a lines plan.

plan and the load waterline in plan can be transferred in HB
pencil from the sketch to this bigger scale drawing. A spline
and possibly a curve or two will be needed for the operation.

Next draw in, freehand, what appeals as sectional shapes
at, say, stations 1, 4 and 7 using the deck lines, rabbet and lwl

as reference points. Now draw in Diagonal 2 (D2) and Buttock 1(B1) with a spline and perhaps a curve. Drawing sections at 1, 4 and 7 will have given clues as to where buttocks and diagonals should be fixed to get the best use out of them.

If the buttock and diagonal which you have just drawn fit the spots, and give a nice curve at the same time, you are on your way. Otherwise adjust the sections and other lines until everything agrees and looks pleasing.

Continue activities by turning your attention to, perhaps, D1 and AWL, which in this case is 6 in (152 mm) below LWL, and then to Buttock 2. There are still only three half-sections drawn but when the work so far suggested has been completed draw in the remaining sections and then D3 and the remaining waterlines, checking and correcting as you go.

If the half-sections are put in over the profile view, as shown, it will ease the task of checking that buttock height in section and profile agree and, if everything is drawn with a sharp HB pencil, rubbing out, and there will be plenty of that, won't be much of a problem.

Before going too far but when the sections look as if they are not likely to alter much more, check that the displacement is about what is wanted. Here a quick sortie into a displacement calculation, Table 9, gives a figure of just over a ton, which is roughly what is required. It is always better to have a boat potentially floating light rather than the other way around.

Drawing a lines plan for a round bilge is a fairly time-consuming business as an alteration in one place tends to alter half-a-dozen other things as well. But stick at it and your patience will be rewarded.

Finally clean up the plan as much as possible and ensure that where lines cross the stations the crossing point is clear. Then dimension the stem and stern profiles as necessary and put in measurements wherever you think the boatbuilder will need them.

There will be a considerable sense of satisfaction when the lines plan is finished, and traced, but on its own, though decorative, it is not much use. What the builder wants is an offset table giving dimensions that he can use for making building

Table 9 Displacement calculation for a round bilge fin keel day sailer

Common interval, 2 ft $1\frac{1}{2}$ in $= 2.125$ ft

Station	Area sq. ft	S.M.	Product	Lever	Product
0	—	1	—	4	—
1	0.34	4	1.36	3	4.08
2	1.00	2	2.00	2	4.00
3	1.95	4	7.80	1	7.80
4	2.43	2	4.86	—	15.88 *Total*
5	2.28	4	9.12	1	9.12
6	1.44	2	2.88	2	5.76
7	0.37	4	1.48	3	4.44
8	—	1	—	4	—
			29.50 *Total*		19.32 *Total*

Displacement in cu. ft $= 2/3 \times 2.125 \times 29.50 = 41.79$
Displacement in lb $= 41.79 \times 64 = 2674$ in salt water (1.19 tons)
Longitudinal centre of buoyancy (lcb) $= \frac{19.32 - 15.88}{29.5} \times 2.125 = 0.25$
That is, lcb is 0.25 ft aft of midships (station 4)

moulds or that allow him to re-draw the vessel full size on the mould loft floor.

Offset table

A typical offset table layout, and one applicable to this boat, is shown in Fig 24. It is all quite straightforward but it helps if one person can measure and read out the offsets from the original lines plan (not the tracing) while someone else writes them down. Fig 25 shows the lines plans and Fig 26 the complete offset table for that 14 ft 6 in cruising dinghy of Chapter 2.

Two other lines plans for round bilge boats are shown in Figs 28 and 30. Fig 27 is a 19 ft (5.8 m) beach boat and Fig 28 its lines plan, in preliminary, rough form. Using the outlines of deck, keel, waterlines, buttocks and diagonal (and making sure

Making the working drawings

Station	0	1	2	3	4	5	6	7	8
				Half-breadths from ℄					
Deck at side						2-11-3			
LWL						2-10-2			
LWL						2-7-3			
Awl						2-0-1			
Rabbet						0-2-4			
				Heights above & below LWL					
Deck at side						1-3-6			
Buttock 1						⁻0-11-2			
Buttock 2						⁻0-6-1			
Rabbet						⁻1-5-3			
Bottom of keel						⁻3-6-4			
				Diagonals from ℄					
Diagonal 1						3-3-4			
Diagonal 2						2-4-0			
Diagonal 3						0-11-0			

Offsets in feet, inches and eighths to outside of planking. The suffix ⁻ in the heights table indicates the offset is below LWL.
Diagonals at 45 deg stations spaced at 2 ft $1\frac{1}{2}$ in.

Fig 24   How the offset table for the day sailer would be set out, with one column filled in.

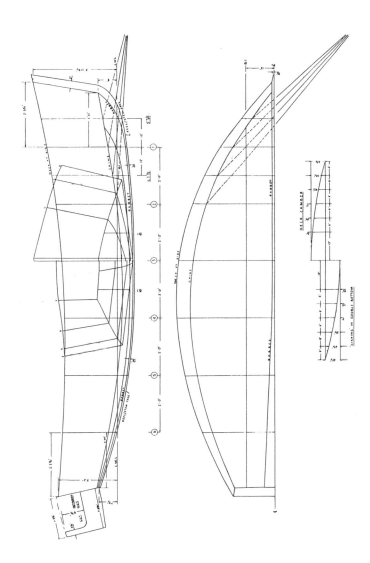

Fig 25   Lines plan of the cruising dinghy.

55

Station	½		1½						
Frame		1		2	3	4	5	6	7
Heights above & below LWL									
Deck at side	2-8-1	2-5-5	2-3-5	2-1-7	1-11-3	1-10-3	1-10-2	1-11-1	2-1-0
Chine	0-6-0	0-3-7	0-2-0	0-0-2	⁻0-2-0	⁻0-2-1	0-0-0	0-3-6	0-8-6
Buttock (B1)		0-0-4	⁻0-2-3	⁻0-3-6	—	—	—	—	—
Rabbet	⁻0-0-4	⁻0-3-3	⁻0-4-6	⁻0-5-6	⁻0-6-4	⁻0-6-3	⁻0-4-1	0-0-7	0-7-7
½ breadths from ₵									
Deck at side	1-1-7	1-10-3	2-5-1	2-10-2	3-4-2	3-5-1	3-1-6	2-6-3	1-5-4
Chine	0-9-2	1-5-2	1-11-5	2-4-4	2-10-1	2-11-3	2-8-4	2-2-1	1-4-7
Rabbet	0-1-0	0-1-0	0-1-0	0-1-0	0-1-0	0-1-2	0-2-2	0-3-3	0-4-4

Offsets in feet, inches and eighths to outside of skin in the heights table. The suffix ⁻ indicates the offset is below LWL.

Fig 26   Offsets for the 14 ft 6 in cruising dinghy.

the engine will go in where needed with a suitable propeller able to swing with adequate tip clearance, the proper lines plan is drawn. A final check on displacement is made and the offset table then drawn up.

We have concentrated almost exclusively so far on smallish boats. After all, the first-time designer is fairly unlikely to try his hand at a big and expensive world girdler or offshore race contender. But everything that has been said applies just as much to large as to small craft and Fig 29 shows a 66 ft (20 m) gaff schooner designed for work in the Arctic. Working sail area is about 2000 sq ft (185 m²). Fig 30 is her lines plan. She has a short counter stern as did the beach boat.

When the offset table is complete, draw the half-sections again to as large a scale as is convenient. Any inaccuracies will then become apparent and a study of the lines plan and, if necessary, some minor re-drawing should put things right. Remember to amend the offset table to take in these corrections.

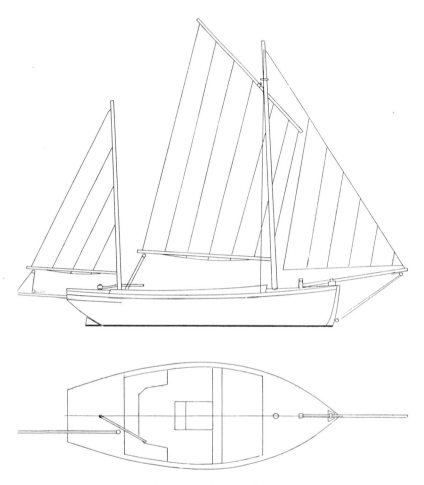

Fig 27   Profile of a 19 ft (5.8 m) beach boat.

On a chine boat, or one with frames rather than steamed timbers, it should help the builder if offsets are given at frames rather than at displacement stations. Though the latter will have to be drawn for displacement and LCB purposes they then would not be used for offsets. To be honest, a minority of builders actually loft the lines. They prefer to fair the vessel as they

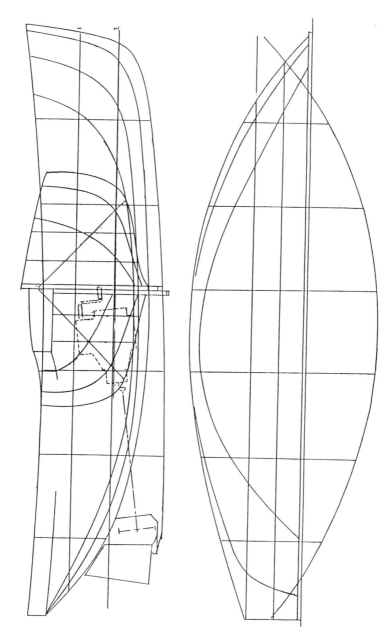

Fig 28   Preliminary lines plan of the beach boat.

Fig 29   The gaff schooner for Arctic exploration.

build it and thus offsets to frames will save them time and save
you money.

Hard chine lines plan

Fig 31 shows the centreboard version of the day sailer in chine
form. Normally, but actually incorrectly, a vee bottom boat is
shown as having straight line sections throughout. Thus only

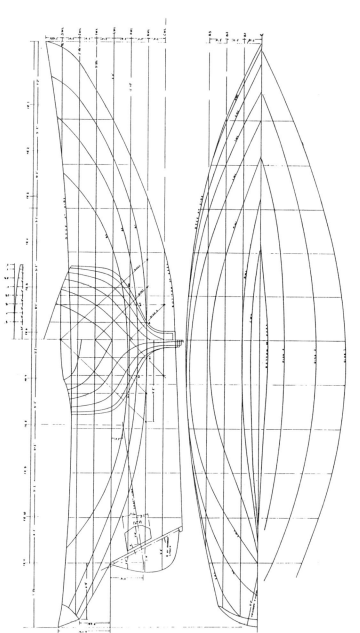

Fig 30 Lines plan of the gaff schooner.

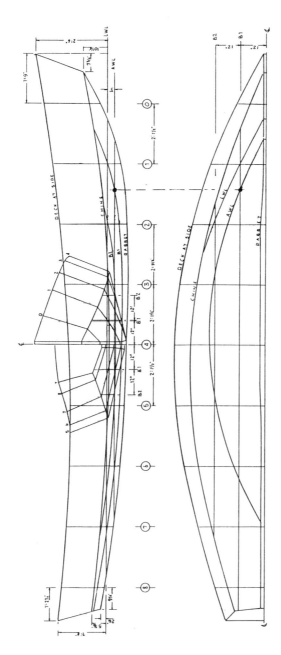

Fig 31 Hard chine version of the 20 ft day sailer with conically developed forward bottom.

the deck, chine and rabbet lines are drawn, with straight lines defining the sections at each station. However, if a piece of card is held so that the bottom edge represents the keel line and the top edge is then twisted into the shape of the chine at the bow, it will be seen that the card between the two is curved, meaning that in fact the sections between chine and keel are curved, not straight.

If this fact is ignored no waterlines, buttocks or diagonals need be drawn and the builder, flexing his muscles and employing a mighty army of cramps, will probably be able to distort the ply, or whatever it is, to conform to the straight frames. He may be forced into producing one or two with curved outer faces, using patterns made on the job.

On the other hand it is possible to predict the shape of the bottom frames together with the appropriate forefoot, having curves that the ply would be glad to follow.

Conic projection

This shape prediction is carried out using a conic projection (Fig 32) and what is derived from it is the correct form for the forward bottom. Elsewhere it is assumed that normal straight line sections will be satisfactory.

Draw in the chine line in plan and profile together with the rabbet in plan. The rabbet in profile can be lightly sketched in as a guide to the desired shape. Next we must find the apexes of the cone in plan and profile that will produce the hoped-for curve, especially round the forefoot. These apexes will always be below lwl, below the centreline in plan and to the right of station 0. Most importantly, the apexes must be in the same vertical line.

Spread a sheet of tracing paper over the lines plan and start experimenting. A generator from the apex in plan view to the intersection of chine line and station will cross the rabbet in plan at some spot. Project this point up to the same generator

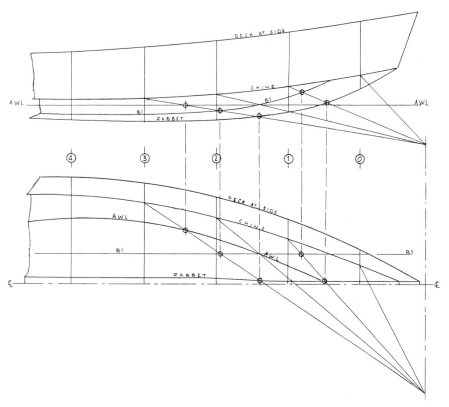

Fig 32   The apexes and generators of the cone.

in profile and its intersection will give a point for the rabbet in profile. Generators are not normally drawn to further aft than midships and in Fig 26 the furthest they go is the chine on station 2.

You might find suitable apexes at the first or second attempt or only after a dozen or more. Move the apexes nearer or further from one another; away from or closer to station 0; and don't give up hope. Keep trying and what seemed ridiculous to begin with will suddenly work out.

When the curve of the forefoot seems satisfactory, attention should be turned to waterlines and buttocks. Their shape is determined by generator crossing points as with the rabbet. Have another look at Fig 32 and all should be revealed.

Only a length of forward bottom will have its shape governed by this conic projection scheme. From about midships aft the sections on this boat will be composed of straight lines because chine and rabbet are running reasonably parallel with little twist between them. On a double-ender though, another, handed, projection is usually needed aft. Fair any lengths where the sections are composed of straight lines into the curved areas in the normal manner. Fig 9 showed the apexes of the generators to form a conic projection for the forward bottom of the cruising dinghy. Work out the apex positions on the initial, small scale lines plan first or you may draw the larger scale lines on the paper such that the apexes of the cones are over the edge of the drawing board.

Centre of effort (CE) and 'lead'

The positioning of the sail plan should now be checked. It was previously stated that the mast should be a little forward of the toe of the keel or centreboard. That was fine but the time has come to place it more definitely than that.

Having first drawn the midships station line, cut out the underwater profile of the boat, including rudder, in tracing paper. Fold it a few times longitudinally, concertina fashion, and then balance it on a compass point. Prick this point through, unfold the paper, and that is the centre of lateral resistance (CLR) and the point about which the craft will pivot.

Then work out the area and centre of area of each sail. A gaff main can be divided into two triangles. The centre of area of a triangle is found by dividing a couple of sides into half and drawing lines to these midway points from their opposite corners (Fig 33). The intersection of the two lines marks the centre of

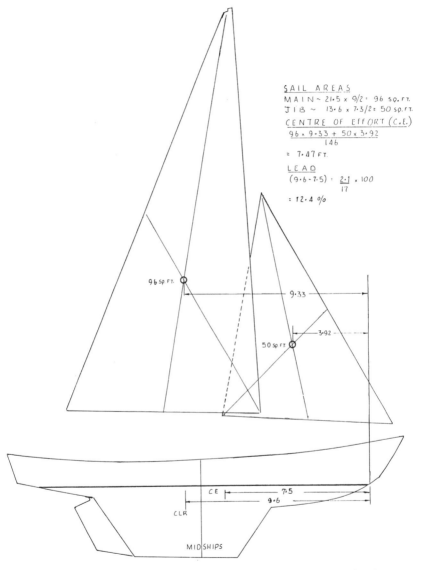

SAIL AREAS
MAIN ~ 21.5 x 9/2 = 96 SQ.FT.
JIB ~ 13.6 x 7.3/2 = 50 SQ.FT.

CENTRE OF EFFORT (C.E.)

$$\frac{96 \times 9.33 + 50 \times 3.92}{146}$$

= 7.47 FT.

LEAD

$$(9.6 - 7.5) = \frac{2.1}{17} \times 100$$

= 12.4 %

96 SQ FT.

9.33

3.92

50 SQ FT.

CE

7.5

9.6

CLR

MIDSHIPS

Fig 33   Working out the position of the centre of effort (CE) and its lead over the centre of lateral resistance (CLR).

area. Now measure the distance of each centre of area from a perpendicular through the forward ending of lwl and multiply that distance by the area of the sail. Add up those figures and divide the total by the total sail area.

This will give the position of the centre of effort (CE) from that forward perpendicular. Mark it on the underwater profile and measure the distance between CLR and CE. This distance divided by the waterline length, and then multiplied by 100, will give the percentage 'lead' of CE over CLR. The lead should be about 12–14 per cent for shallow hull, fin keel or centreboard craft; about 10 per cent for deeper more traditional yachts; and about 8 per cent for cruising yachts of classic form.

4 Motor boat design

Chapters 1 to 3 have concentrated almost exclusively on sailing craft, so now we had better redress the balance and have a look at motor boats whilst reassuring those interested in power who have slogged through those opening chapters that their time has not been wasted. The mechanics of drawing lines plans, fairing them, and working out weights and displacement calculations are precisely the same, whatever type of boat is being designed. It is only the hull shape that may be different and even that is not always the case. The underwater form of a low speed motor boat will be similar to that of a sailing hull simply because with a limited amount of power available, whether from sails or engine, the hull has to offer as little resistance to moving through the water as possible.

Figs 34 and 35 show an example of the type. A river cruiser 27 ft 6 in by 10 ft 3 in (8.4 m × 3.1 m) with a displacement of 3 tons, she has a 10 hp motor to give a top speed of around $6\frac{1}{2}$ knots. Waterline length is 25 ft (7.6 m). The transom is just clear of the water and the buttocks are running up in gentle curves to clear the wash from around her stern with as little fuss as possible. Round bilge configuration would have been a slight advantage from the easy running point of view but she was built in aluminium alloy where using the material in sheet

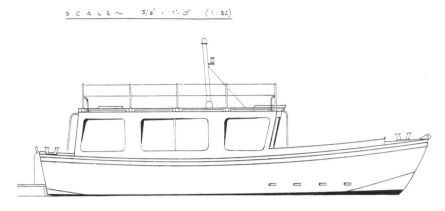

Fig 34   Above water profile of the 27 ft 6 in river cruiser.

form saves a fair amount of money; a consideration not to be sneezed at.

But when we grandly talk of low speed motor boats, what do we really mean? When does low speed become something else? Well, before answering that there is one term that must be understood.

Speed/length ratio

Here boat speed in knots (V) is compared with waterline length in feet (L). $V/\sqrt{L}$ is speed/length ratio. Thus a vessel 25 ft on the waterline at, say, 6 knots has a speed/length ratio of: $6/\sqrt{25}$ or 6/5 which is 1:2. At 10 knots her speed/length ratio is $10/\sqrt{25}$, giving an answer of 2. A 300 ft ferry at 20 knots has a speed/length ratio of: $20/\sqrt{300}$ which is 1:15, and so on.

This principally allows us to define the category of boat which will apply to a particular vessel, and so to design a hull that will

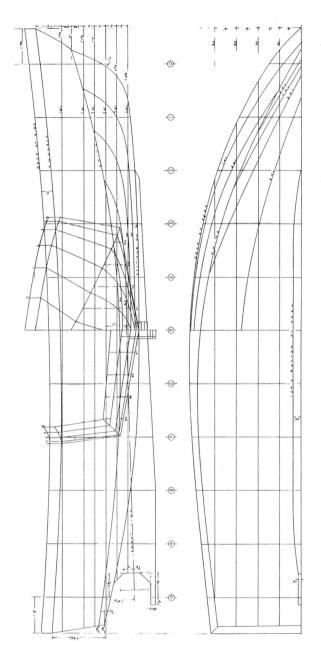

Fig 35 Lines plan of the river cruiser. Like all other single and double chine vessels in this book, the forward sections are conically developed.

suit this category. For this purpose we can define the categories as follows:

- *Low speed* – up to a speed/length ratio of about 1.6
- *Medium speed* – having a speed/length ratio of between 1.6 and 3
- *High speed* – with a speed/length ratio above 3

It will be appreciated that by using speed/length ratio all sorts of sizes and speeds can be neatly corralled together. A motor boat 30 ft on the waterline and doing 20 knots has a speed/length ratio of 3.6 and so can be classed as a high speed vessel but a 300-footer at the same 20 knots is running at a speed/length ratio of 1.15 and so is a low speed type, to be designed as such. For her to be considered high speed she would have to be doing:

$V/\sqrt{L} = 3$ (or more)

$V = 3 \times \sqrt{L}$ or $V = 3 \times 17.3$

$V = 52$ knots and even then would be comparatively slower than the 30-footer which was running at a speed/length ratio of 3.6.

Wave making

As a boat moves along it shoulders water aside and in doing so makes waves. One set of these pressure waves runs diagonally out from the bow and another, less noticeably, from the stern. A further, more important set, runs transversely along the vessel's sides with a crest visible at the bow followed by a trough and then another crest which may be, depending on the craft's speed, somewhere within the length of the hull or out past the stern. On a big boat especially, there may be several crests in the vessel's length initially but as speed rises the waves will lengthen until there is a crest at the bow and another at the stern and then only a single visible crest near the bow. The rest of the wave system will have passed astern. It takes power to

Table 10 Wave length depends on boat speed

Speed (knots)	Length (feet)	Speed (knots)	Length (feet)
6	20.0	12	80.1
7	27.2	14	109.6
8	35.6	16	142.4
9	45.0	20	222.5
10	55.6	25	347.7
11	67.3	30	500.6

make these waves and a heavy, bulky craft will make bigger and deeper waves than some light, lean counterpart.

The distance between wave crests, or the length of the waves, is governed entirely by boat speed, Table 10. So a 30 ft (9.1 m) boat at, say, 7 knots is creating a transverse wave system, the distance between whose crests (27.2 ft) is less than the length of the boat. At some speed between 7 and 8 knots the aft crest will have moved astern of the vessel and it will move further and further astern as speed rises. At, for instance, 10 knots the wave length between crests will be over 55 ft. The speed when the wave length is the same as the length of the hull is known as the vessel's displacement or hull speed. On a 40-footer it would be somewhere between 8 and 9 knots; on an 80-footer, 12 knots and so on. Specifically, the hull speed occurs at a speed/length ratio of 1.34. Any type of boat from dinghy to supertanker makes the same length of wave at the same speed. It is only the wave size that alters with vessel weight and form.

What happens in practice is shown in Fig 36. A boat about 21 ft (6.4 m) on the waterline is shown travelling first at about 6 knots. Table 10 indicates that at that speed the wave length is 20 ft and so the vessel is nicely supported by crests at bow and stern and will ride pretty well level. The lower sketch assumes speed has risen to 9 knots. Wave length is now 45 ft. The bow is still supported by the forward wave crest but the stern is in a hollow. The boat is trimming horribly bows-up and is essentially trying to travel uphill – a power-absorbing pursuit.

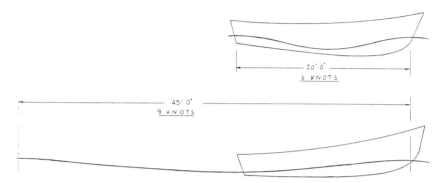

Fig 36   As boat speed increases the wave system becomes longer and the vessel trims by the stern.

Motor boat hulls

The usual, though not quite the only, way of overcoming this excessively bows-up attitude is to have a hull with a wide, buoyant transom and stern sections against which the oncoming water can exert a good upwards push. The boat will be presenting a wedge-shaped profile to this torrent with the result that it tends to lift the deepest part – the stern – and so reduces the high bow posture.

It can be imagined that the river cruiser of Figs 34 and 35 would present a sorry picture when attempting to reach velocities beyond those of her displacement speed. She would sit down with bows supported by the forward wave crest and general attitude such that her aft buttocks were lying flat on the wave slope.

Considerably better would be the small steel workboat of Fig 37. Though not designed for high speeds her run aft is reasonably flat and combined with an immersed transom she would travel at a steep but just about acceptable angle such that the oncoming water could act to lift her stern provided she had sufficient power installed.

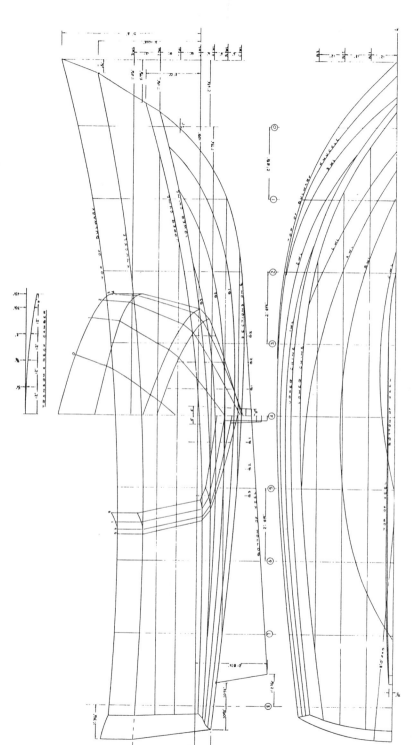

Fig 37   Lines plan of a 25 ft steel workboat capable of moderate speeds.

Better still in the pursuit of speed is a hull form where the aft buttocks run pretty well parallel to the designed waterline and the transom width is as great as anywhere in the boat, or nearly so. A slight taper towards the stern from the point of widest beam looks best but slight is the operative word. Fig 38 shows these features in a 27 ft × 9 ft (8.2 m × 2.7 m) speedboat hull designed for about 35 knots. Though not very apparent there is a small, flat area in the bottom aft, to promote early planing. Incidentally, a boat is said to be planing when the sides above the chine and the transom are running dry. Topsides forward should be given good flare to help promote a dry deck.

For good lift qualities curves both longitudinally and transversely are best avoided. Thus the buttock lines from somewhere near midships right back to the transom should be flat, too. A 'flattie' motor boat would be fine for messing about, or even dashing around at speed on calm waters and would plane very early but would be skittish in strong winds, there being virtually nothing of the boat in the water at high speeds. In rough water she would beat herself to pieces in no time at all. So practical boat hulls have to be given some vee or deadrise. The greater the vee the greater the loss of lift but the better the seakeeping qualities and, eventually, high deadrise angles can lead to improved high speed performance because they allow gradually reducing waterline beam. But more of that in the sections on beam and spray rails that follow.

To sum up, boats intended for medium speeds are designed with one eye on reasonable low speed qualities. That is, gradually rising buttocks aft and only quite lightly immersed transoms allow the water to clear the stern without too much power-sapping turbulence. Fast boats, on the other hand, are drawn with no consideration other than speed. Running lines aft are pretty well parallel to the designed waterline with a consequently deeply immersed transom. This drags a mess of water behind it at low speeds with dire effects on low speed performance.

A compromise form is shown in Figs 39 and 40. This is a medium speed cruiser – about 12 knots maximum which on a waterline length of 32 ft 6 in (9.9 m) gives a speed/length ratio

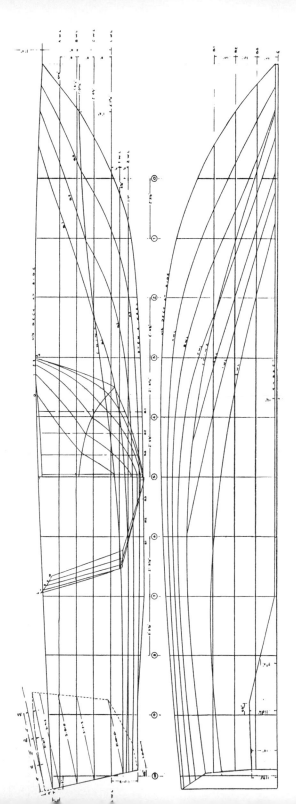

Fig 38   Lines plan of the 28 ft speedboat with single chine and designed for a speed of something like 35 knots.

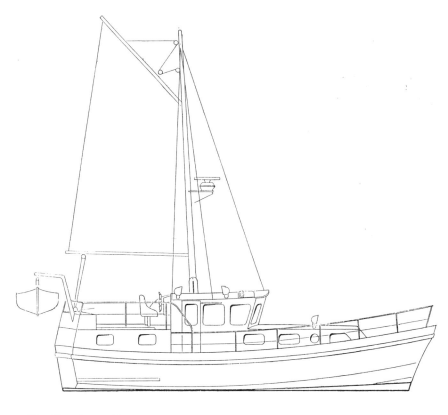

Fig 39   A medium speed cruiser with 12 knots or so maximum.

of 2.1. Here the aft buttocks start by running upwards in the conventional manner but then straighten out to give a perfectly flat surface towards the transom. As the boat trims stern down in her climb up the speed range, this surface becomes angled down into the water stream and acts as a wedge to lift the stern. Such a system works fine after trials afloat to find the best size and angle for the wedge, which may subsequently be incorporated into the bottom shell or remain as separate (port and starboard) planted-on wedges. However, it can be imagined

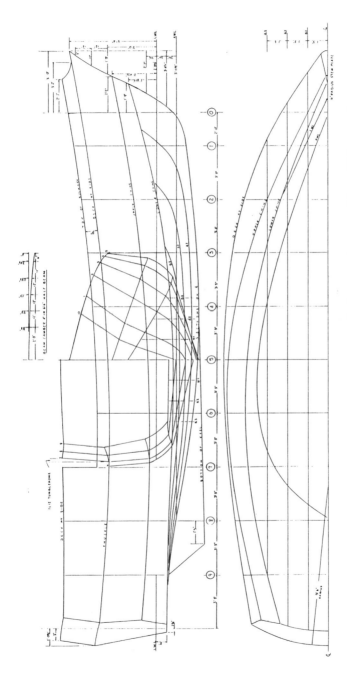

Fig 40 The medium speed cruiser with running lines aft flattened to provide a lifting surface which helps counteract excessive stern-down trim.

that wedges continue to perform until they are parallel with the waterline and thus no longer effective. If they had been angled down towards the stern to begin with they may cause the boat to trim down by the bow at speed, which would be dangerous and inefficient. A bows-up trim of between 2 and 4 degrees is usually the best all-round attitude.

In all cases a chine form is preferable and is vital for fast boats to keep the topsides above the chine running as dry as possible and thus lessening frictional resistance. A chine rail (Fig 41) materially assists. The greater the area of surface that is wetted by the sea, the more the power that is needed to drive the boat along. Where a double chine is used, as here on a medium speed vessel, to soften the abrupt change in shape that occurs with a single chine and so to lessen resistance, the rail runs above the upper chine. With round bilge form, a chine rail is absolutely necessary, running just above the turn of the bilge aft which should have as tight a radius as possible.

Many outdrives and bigger outboards incorporate some form of tilt mechanism where the angle of thrust from the propeller can be selected. Using such an arrangement alters the trim of

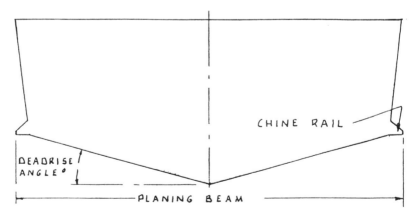

Fig 41   Definitions of some terms used when describing a motor boat's hull.

the boat and so helps in attaining the best running trim. Transom flaps can also be useful in controlling trim.

Low wave making types

At the beginning of this section we mentioned the length of the pressure wave caused by the boat's passage being governed solely by speed but its depth from crest to trough being related to its weight and form. If the wave depth was slight, the vessel would not have such a steep hill to climb. It thus follows that a lean and light craft would have fewer problems in achieving respectable speeds without bad trim problems on the way than a bluff heavyweight. This applies, of course, to motor craft as well as sailing vessels. With the latter, a conventional yacht, with outside ballast and power limited by the fact that it heels and loses power as the wind increases, can never overcome the trim problem. But something like a windsurfer, with a lightweight and svelte hull and with crew weight disposed such that it has the maximum effect on reducing heel, can very easily power through the pressure wave barrier. So too can, say, a lightweight catamaran where twin hulls resist undue heel and loss of power.

With motor boats it is very rare to see examples that take advantage of the possibility but, between World Wars I and II, Camper and Nicholsons built a range of sleek round bilge launches about 50 ft (15.2 m) in length with a narrow beam of about 8 ft (2.4 m). Constructed lightly in timber, these craft could manage 20 knots with a 100 hp engine; a very respectable speed/length ratio of 2.8 achieved by using a slim, low wave-making hull.

As another example, using lightweight aluminium alloy construction, Universal Shipyards built some 26 ft (7.9 m) launches having a displacement of about 1.3 tons in the 50s and early 60s. With a 65 hp installed, these craft could manage 22 knots – a triumph for light displacement. This speed/length ratio of about 4.4 was achieved on a round bilge hull quite far removed from the ideal planing boat form, being simply bent up from what was essentially one sheet of alloy per side.

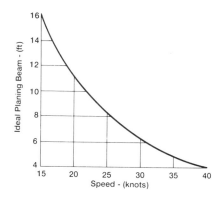

Fig 42   Ideal planing form beam for a 25 ft fast motor boat at various speeds.

Beam and lcb

Tank test work allows us to work out the ideal planing beam for any fast motor boat if we know its intended speed, displacement, deadrise, waterline length and position of the lcg. Fig 42 shows the result of a calculation for a vessel 25 ft (7.6 m) on the waterline with a displacement of four tons and with its lcg 55 per cent of the waterline length aft of the forward waterline ending; deadrise is 15 degrees.

So if 20 knots had been the designed operating speed, the average chine beam (Fig 42) between midships and the transom should be around 11 ft (3.3 m). If 30 knots had been the aim, a beam of just over 6 ft (1.8 m) would be more appropriate. All this probably usefully shows is that the usual overall length/overall beam ratio of 3:1 is about right for general use but that if really high operating speeds are anticipated reducing the beam is an advantage.

The lcb and lcg on virtually all motor boats should be about 55 per cent of the waterline length aft of the forward waterline ending.

Deadrise

This is the angle the bottom makes with the horizontal from its centreline ending (Fig 41 again) just as it is on sailing craft. In fact the angle is much the same, too, 15 degrees at midships being an average sort of figure, rising considerably at the bow and dropping slightly at the stern.

On fast boats the deadrise is often increased quite a lot in the interests of soft riding in rough water. It would be classed as a deep vee if that rise of floor were 22 degrees or more at midships. In such a case, deadrise at the transom would rarely be less than 18 degrees or so, while at the bow it would certainly be more but the chine would not lift as much as it does on lower midships deadrise boats.

Spray rails

On these deep vees, an interesting phenomenon occurs at speed. All fast boats lift bodily in the water above speed/length ratios of 3, or thereabouts, as the dynamic lift given by the water rushing past the bottom really takes hold. Most high speed craft sport spray rails running along the bottom to give a certain amount of lift and to deflect spray away from areas of the bottom that might otherwise be wetted. With steeply vee'd sections the time comes as speeds rise and the boat lifts in consequence that one set of spray rails deflects water so completely that the area of bottom above them runs dry. This, in effect, defines a new and narrower waterline beam which, as was mentioned in the previous section, is desirable at high speeds.

Eventually, of course, the next, lower set of spray rails may take over to create an even narrower beam and so on. This does not normally happen on craft with more modest deadrise angles because the water deflected by the rails simply forms again on the hull above the rails (Fig 43).

Spray rails are normally of triangular form with their bottom faces horizontal. They start at the chine in the form of

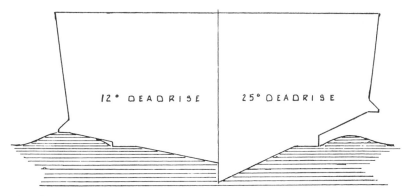

Fig 43 A spray rail can make water break away from the bottom of a deep vee hull but generally not on craft with shallower vees.

chine rails and are then set in pairs running, on modestly vee'd boats, from just aft of midships to as near the bow as can be managed without their fitting becoming too difficult. On deep vees they run full length, though near the keel where they stand no chance of defining a new beam they can be shortened in the interests of reducing wetted surface.

There is no need for these rails on low and medium speed craft where they can achieve very little of practical value but simply increase wetted surface.

Speed prediction

Table 11 gives bhp (brake horsepower) figures based on the waterline length and displacement of the craft. Thus, for instance, a motor boat 20 ft (6.1 m) on the waterline and displacing 1.5 tons would require 24 bhp to do 9 knots, provided she had a 'transom and flat stern' form. Translated into the categories we devised, these type headings would be, first, low speed form (canoe stern), then medium speed form and, finally, high speed form. The answers will be wrong if the hull shape is not of the

Table 11 The required brake horsepower needed for various speeds can be determined when waterline length and displacement are known

Type of stern		Canoe stern		Transom and flat stern			Transom and very flat stern or chine form						V-chine or stepped	
		Speed in knots												
Length	Tons	5	6	7	8	9	10	11	12	13	14	15	16	17
20 ft	0.5	1.0	1.7	2.9	4.7	7.2	10	12	14	17	19	22		
	1.0	1.8	3.6	6.6	10.8	16	20	24	28	33	39	44		
	1.5	2.6	5.7	11	17	24	30	36	43	50	58	67		
	2.0	3.1	8.0	15	22	32	40	48	57	67	77	89		
	3.0	3.7	12	24	33	48	59	72	85	100	116	134		
25 ft	2.0	2.4	5.0	10	17	25	34	42	50	59	68	78		
	3.0	3.0	6.5	15	26	37	48	61	74	88	102	115		
	4.0	4.0	8.7	22	36	50	64	84	100	117	136	155		
	5.0	5.0	12	28	46	65	85	105	125	146	170	196		
30 ft	1.5	1.6	2.9	4.9	7.4	11	15	23	31	37	43	50	57	
	2.0	1.9	3.6	6.4	10.4	15	22	32	42	50	58	67	76	
	3.0	2.5	5.0	9.7	17	26	36	48	62	75	87	100	114	
	4.0	3.0	6.4	13	26	37	51	64	83	100	116	133	152	
	5.0	3.3	7.7	16	32	46	66	80	104	125	145	167	190	
	6.0	3.5	8.8	19	39	56	79	96	125	150	174	200	227	
	8.0	4.0	11	26	51	74	105	128	166	200	232	267	303	
40 ft	4.0	2.8	5.2	8.5	13	20	28	39	53	67	84	97	110	124
	6.0	3.5	7.0	12	20	34	50	55	89	105	126	144	164	186
	8.0	4.0	8.4	15	26	47	73	94	119	145	168	193	219	248
	10.0	4.4	9.9	18	33	61	92	122	149	180	210	242	274	310
	12.0	4.6	11	21	40	75	110	146	179	217	252	290	329	372
	14.0	5.0	12	24	46	87	128	170	208	252	294	338	384	434
	16.0	5.2	13	27	53	100	147	195	238	289	336	387	439	465
	18.0	5.6	14	30	59	112	165	219	268	325	378	435	494	558
	20.0	5.9	15	33	66	125	183	244	298	361	420	484	548	620
50 ft	8.0	4.1	7.2	13	19	28	39	55	74	99	124	150	177	205
	10.0	4.6	7.9	15	23	35	53	76	100	130	162	193	228	257
	12.0	5.0	8.8	17	27	42	66	96	122	164	199	243	283	309
	14.0	5.3	9.6	20	30	49	82	116	155	198	243	286	330	360
	16.0	5.6	10	21	34	56	98	137	183	234	278	327	376	412
	18.0	5.8	11	23	38	63	112	168	212	270	313	368	423	463
	20.0	6.0	12	25	41	70	128	192	248	300	348	408	470	515
	25.0	6.5	13	30	50	87	164	240	312	375	435	510	588	643
	30.0	7.0	14	34	57	105	197	288	374	450	522	612	705	775
	35.0	8.0	15	37	66	123	230	336	437	525	609	715	823	900

type specified. These are calm water power requirements and can probably be doubled for practical purposes.

The table can also be used as a guide to auxiliary power on yachts with some caution. A yacht may have considerably more windage than a motor boat due to her masts and rigging (though that wouldn't be so with those motor boats where box is piled upon box in the way of coachroofs, flying bridges, radar masts and so forth) and will almost certainly have greater wetted surface with her ballast keel.

For speeds higher than those covered by Table 11 a formula can be used. This is:

$$V = 124.7 \times \frac{P^{0.551}}{W^{0.476}}$$

where V is boat speed in mph; W is displacement in pounds; and P is shaft horsepower (about 10 per cent less than brake horse-power).

As an example let's take a boat with a displacement of 2000 lb with 150 shp installed. The sum then works out as:

$$V = 124.7 \times \frac{150^{0.551}}{2000^{0.476}}$$

That is: $V = 124.7 \times 15.8/37.3$. $V = 52.8$ mph or $52.8 \times 5280/6080 = 45.9$ knots, there being 5280 ft in a statute mile and 6080 ft in a nautical mile.

The formula can be turned round to find power, given a displacement and required speed. Thus:

$$P = \sqrt[0.551]{\frac{W^{0.476} \times V}{124.7}}$$

Put in the speed required (V, in mph) and you have your answer.

Propellers

The best people to advise on propellers are the manufacturers. This advice, based on experience as well as calculation, will be free if you order from them but it is often useful to have a good idea of the likely diameter from early on in the design process. The aperture for the prop can then be drawn with confidence. Tip clearance between hull and propeller blade should be at least 20 per cent of the diameter. So a 20 in diameter propeller would need a gap of 4 in between blade tips and hull.

A useful guide is as follows: a propeller should turn at between 80 and 100 rpm for every mph of boat speed. Hence a craft designed for 8 mph (6.9 knots) would be happy and efficient with a prop turning at somewhere around 800 rpm. This implies a large diameter, as will be seen, which would seriously hamper progress on a sailing boat with auxiliary engine but would be proper on a motor launch. There is no requirement to stick closely to any answer provided by that guide but it is worth keeping at the back of your mind. In general it is more efficient to accelerate a large column of water slowly than a small column fast.

Table 12 gives a guide to likely prop diameters based on propeller rpm and brake horsepower. For example, let us suppose we have a 20 bhp engine which develops this power at 2500 rpm. Possible reduction gears are 1.5:1, 2:1 and 3:1. What would be suitable propeller diameters?

With 1.5:1 reduction the prop will be turning at 1666 rpm. At 20 hp that gives about 13 in as a suitable diameter. Assuming 2:1, the prop would be turning at 1250 rpm and the diameter would be around 15 in and with 3:1 reduction and 833 rpm, 19 in diameter might fill the bill. And so on.

The choice of associated propeller pitch, which is governed by slip, prop rpm and boat speed is best left to the experts (ie the manufacturers).

Tunnel sterns

In the case of very shoal-draught motor boats, it may be impossible to swing a decent propeller under the hull. There are

Table 12 Suitable propeller diameters for various powers of engine coupled with propeller rpm

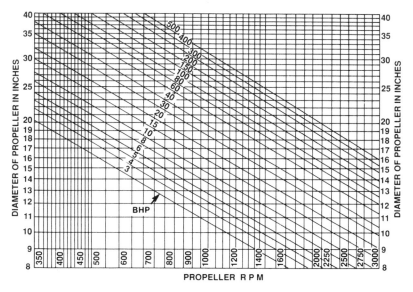

two possible solutions. The first is to sweep the bottom up, rather as in Fig 40 and tuck the propeller under the high point of the hull. The disadvantage of this is that it loses a lot of buoyancy aft, which may push the lcb rather far forward.

The alternative is to employ a tunnel stern. Here a normal hull shape is drawn and the propeller(s) housed in partial tunnels set into the bottom. Figs 44 and 45 show this in practice on a 60 ft × 18 ft (18.3 m × 5.5 m) ferry where loaded draught was restricted to 2 ft 6 in (0.8 m). As can be seen, this was a twin-screw vessel. Fig 46 gives the basic shape of a typical tunnel which can be planted in almost any hull. The propeller, incidentally, should be a snug fit in the tunnel with blade tip clearance of not more than about 1 in (25 mm). The top of the tunnel may

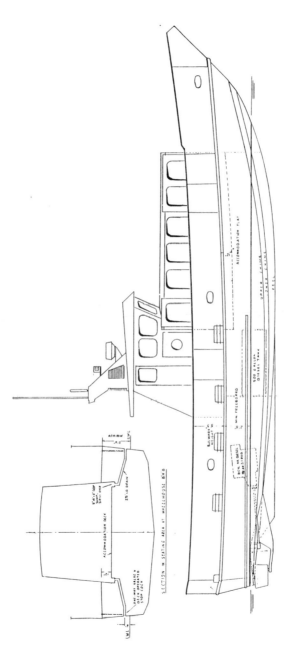

Fig 44 A 60 ft passenger ferry.

Motor boat design

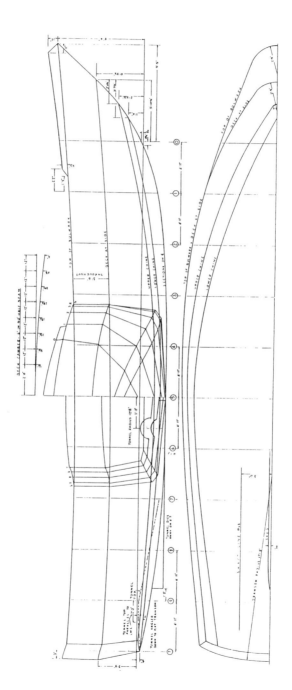

Fig 45 Lines plan of ferry with tunnel stern.

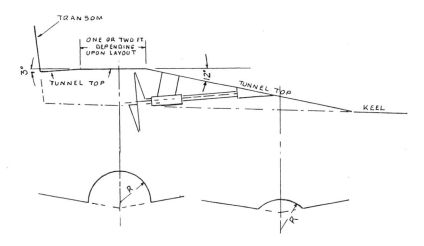

Fig 46   The basic form of a tunnel stern.

be as high as the load waterline or even slightly above it but
its exit should be submerged or the propeller may suck in air
as well as water when going astern, with obvious effects on
performance.

5 Resistance, sail plans and hull balance

In Chapter 4 we looked at the habit boats have of producing power-sapping waves as they move through the water. That chapter dwelt mainly on speeds above displacement speeds which, to jog your memory, is when a boat is travelling at a speed/length ratio of 1.34. But wave-making occurs at all speeds and its resistance to motion is termed wave-making or residuary resistance. The other component of total resistance is frictional resistance and is caused by the friction between water and hull, plus all its appendages such as rudders, keels, centreboards, propellers, shafts and so forth.

Resistance

What follows may seem rather high-flown but it does have practical implications, which will be revealed in the following sections.

Fig 47 shows resistance curves for a typical motor boat. Curves for a centreboard sailing vessel would be of similar form

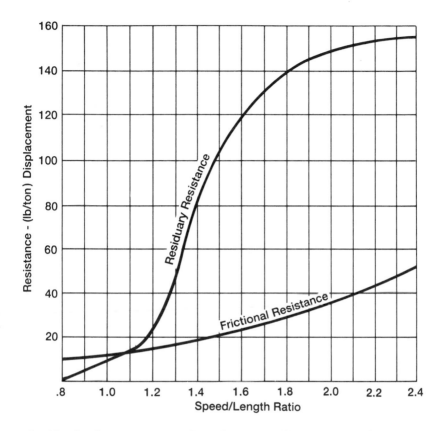

Fig 47   Resistance curves for a boat travelling at speed/length ratios of up to 2.4. This covers most sailing types and some powered vessels, particularly commercial craft.

but a deep-keel yacht would have a greater frictional component. It will be seen that the proportion of total resistance contributed by frictional and residuary (wave-making) resistance depends on speed/length ratio. Initially, frictional resistance is the greater absorber of power but at a speed/length ratio of about 1.05 their effects are about equal and above that ratio wave-making becomes the predominant feature. Resistance is given in lb per ton of displacement and can be converted to horsepower in the formula $BHP = 2 \times R \times V/550$, where R is resistance in pounds and V is the speed of the vessel in feet per second. Multiply knots by 1.68 to get ft/s. Thus 8 knots is 8×1.68, or 13.44 ft/s.

Looking at those curves total resistance at a speed/length ratio of 0.8 (4 knots on a 25-footer) is about 9 lb for friction and 2 lb for wave-making or residuary resistance. The grand total, then, is 11 pounds per ton and if the boat's displacement were 5 tons, total resistance would be $11 \times 5 = 55$ lb. Translated into brake horsepower that is:

$$BHP = \frac{2 \times 55 \times 4 \times 1.68}{550} = 1.34$$

'4×1.68' is converting 4 knots into ft/s.

At a speed/length ratio of 1.4 (roughly hull speed and representing 7 knots on our 25-footer), frictional resistance is 19 lb/ton and residuary, about 80 lb/ton. Totalling these numbers we get 99 lb/ton or $99 \times 5 = 495$ lb for a five-tonner. So:

$$BHP = \frac{2 \times 495 \times 7 \times 1.68}{550} = 21.2$$

Thus to achieve a modest 3 knots increase in speed, power requirements have gone up nearly 16 times. These are calm water figures, of course.

Length clearly plays a vital part in resistance and consequent power requirements. At the same speed/length ratio boats of similar form will have roughly equal resistance per ton of displacement. That is, a 25-footer at 5 knots, say; a 49-footer at 7 knots; and a boat 81 ft on the waterline at 9 knots would require the same horsepower per ton of displacement though speed has nearly doubled.

When thinking of how to get the best out of the size of boat being considered, there is not a lot that can be done in the design stage to reduce frictional resistance. The shape giving least wetted area for a given displacement is the arc of a circle but that is not a practical form for the sections except, perhaps, on multi-hulls where rolling and heeling are controlled by the existence of the two hulls. A chine may marginally assist a motor boat even at these low speed/length ratios and it is sensible to keep the length of exposed propeller shaft as short as possible, but really we'd do better concentrating on wave-making. Here we can influence the outcome quite considerably by drawing a hull where the fore and aft distribution of displacement best suits the likely speed/length ratio. This is done by seeking guidance from what is known as the prismatic coefficient.

Prismatic coefficient

This is the ratio of the immersed volume to the area of the midship section multiplied by waterline length. A fine C_p (prismatic coefficient) indicates a full midship section, implying that the displacement is concentrated around midships. A full C_p, on the other hand, suggests a fine midships section and full ends. This is the formula:

$$C_p = \frac{\text{Disp.} \times 35}{L \times A_m}$$

where displacement is in tons and the multiplier, 35, converts into cubic feet; L is waterline length, in feet; and A_m is the area of the midships section below the waterline, in square feet. As with all such formulae, the imperial measurements can be replaced by metric units to give the same answer.

Just as an example we could work out the sum for that 60 ft passenger ferry of Figs 44 and 45. Displacement there was 32 tons, waterline length 49.2 ft and area of midships section 37.2 sq ft. So putting those numbers into the formula:

$$C_p = \frac{32 \times 35}{49.2 \times 37.2}$$

$$C_p = 0.61$$

Design service speed was around 10 knots, giving a speed/length ratio of 1.4.

Fig 48 shows the ideal prismatic coefficient at various speed/length ratios and it will be seen that for the ferry and a ratio of 1.4, the C_p would ideally be 0.63, so that considering the many practical restraints inherent in a shoal draught commercial vessel our 0.61 isn't too far out.

That aiming for the best prismatic coefficient is not just an exercise in one-upmanship is shown by trials carried out on four 65 ft (19.8 m) fishing boats, Table 13. All except the Admiralty boat had a displacement of about 71 tons and with a waterline length of 62 ft and speed of 9 knots, speed/length ratio was 1.14. Glancing at Fig 48, it appears that the ideal C_p for such a ratio would be about 0.54 and that indeed was what *Silver Searcher* had. This enabled her to reach 9 knots with only 75 bhp. The others needed over 100 bhp for the same speed and in two cases considerably over.

You might also have noticed that the low prismatic of *Silver Searcher* has led to her having a half-angle of entrance at the waterline of 9 degrees compared with the other's angle of over 20 degrees. This angle is the one the load waterline makes with the centreline at its forward ending; half angle because the

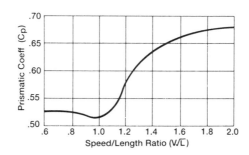

Fig 48   Optimum prismatic coefficients at different speed/length ratios.

Table 13 Details of four similar fishing boats evaluated against each other. From the standpoint of hull efficiency *Silver Searcher* was the clear winner with her low prismatic coefficient and small half angle of entrance

Feature	Admiralty type 65 ft MFV	Original G L Watson design	Modified G L Watson design Silver Scout	Herring board design Silver Searcher
Length overall	64 ft 6 in	65 ft 0 in	65 ft 0 in	65 ft 0 in
Length waterline	60 ft 0 in	62 ft 0 in	62 ft 0 in	62 ft 0 in
Maximum beam	17 ft 10 in	17 ft 10 in	17 ft 10 in	17 ft 10 in
Draught forward	4 ft 3 in	4 ft 9 in	4 ft 9 in	5 ft $8\frac{1}{2}$ in
Draught aft	7 ft 0 in	7 ft 3 in	7 ft 3 in	7 ft $2\frac{1}{2}$ in
Displacement	50 tons	71 tons	71 tons	71.5 tons
Block coefficient	0.35	0.383	0.378	0.359
Prismatic coeff.	0.62	0.645	0.612	0.537
Midship coeff.	0.56	0.594	0.617	0.675
Bhp for 9 knots	120	123	105	75
$\frac{1}{2}$ *angle of entrance at w/line*	23 deg	26 deg	21 deg	9 deg

angle is measured on one side only. Table 14 gives the desirable half angle of entrance at various speed/length ratios.

Prismatic coefficient is just as important on sailing craft as on powered vessels. A cruising yacht is reckoned to travel at a speed/length ratio of 1.0 to 1.15 as an average while a more racing orientated vessel might increase these ratios to 1.25 or 1.35. Such figures would suggest prismatics of about 0.53 to 0.55 and 0.58 to 0.63 respectively. A happy compromise would be a prismatic of 0.58. This would be fine if all yachts had canoe bodies and standard fin keels, but keels may be long or short, fat or thin, deep or shallow or any combination. This has an unsettling effect on the formula. Help is at hand, though, for an American naval architect, J E Paris, from a study of many successful designs, developed a curve showing the best relationship between prismatic coefficient and what is called lateral plane coefficient.

Table 14 Desirable half angles of entrance at various speed/length ratios

Speed/length ratio	Half angle of entrance (deg)
0.5	30
0.6	26
0.7	22
0.8	18
0.9	14
1.0 to 2.0	10

This coefficient is the ratio of the lateral plane in profile (including the rudder, other than remotely hung spade rudders, but excluding centreboards) and the circumscribing rectangle. The latter is waterline length multiplied by maximum draught.

Going back to that 20 ft day sailer (Fig 22) the lateral plane area is 33 sq ft; the waterline length, 17 ft; and maximum draught, 3.5 ft. Work that out; C_{1p} is lateral plane coefficient.

$$C_{1p} = \frac{33}{17 \times 3.5}$$

$$C_{1p} = 0.55$$

An approximation of the Paris curve is given in Fig 49 and so what is needed now is the prismatic coefficient for that 20-footer.

That is worked out easily enough. Displacement is 1.19 tons; waterline length 17 ft; and midship section underwater area, 4.86 sq ft.

$$C_p = \frac{1.19 \times 35}{17 \times 4.86}$$

$$C_p = 0.5$$

The midships section area can, of course, be taken direct from the displacement calculation corrected for scale, if necessary, and doubled because only half areas were used then.

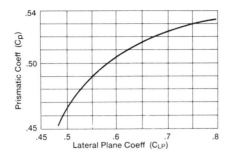

Fig 49   Desirable prismatic coefficients plotted against lateral plane coefficients.

Back to the Paris curve for prismatic and lateral plane coefficient, which shows that for a C_{lp} of 0.55 the optimum C_p would be about 0.49. Since ours was 0.5 that can be considered satisfactory.

Just before embarking on one more consideration of hull form, that of balance when heeled, it might be a relief to have a brief and possibly contentious look at the rig of yachts.

The rig

No apologies are offered for the fact that the various sail plans given throughout this book are all, by today's standards, a bit odd. Gaffs, lugs, sliding gunters . . . and not a single example of the omnipresent Bermudian or triangular main set-up. For those, all one has to do is to look round the nearest marina. There they are in their hundreds, with their associated hi-tech masts and rigging. Yet is this concentration on a single type really justified?

For going to windward, high aspect-ratio rigs are efficient and, within reason, the higher the ratio the better. Aspect-ratio

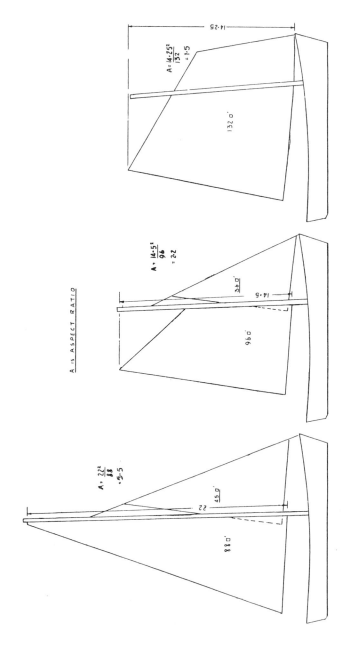

Fig 50 Three different rigs of the same area but very different aspect-ratios. The right-hand sketch shows a dipping lug.

is the length of the luff of the sail squared and then divided by the sail area; Fig 50 shows the aspect-ratio on various rigs. But sailing trials on full-size craft and wind tunnel tests seem to show that while a high aspect-ratio is beneficial when the craft is driving to windward with hardened sheets, as the vessel heads off and sheets are eased it becomes steadily less important. With the boom off at about 35 degrees to the centreline an aspect-ratio as low as 1 is quite acceptable. This is the sort of figure that might be achieved with gaff, sprit and lugsail rigs.

Should a rig be selected solely on the grounds of its better windward performance while disregarding its complexity, cost and, dare one say, uninspiring looks? Be that as it may, there are craft on which high aspect-ratio rigs are nearly always justified and these are the speedsters of this world: racing multi-hulls, some lightweight dinghies, ice yachts, land yachts and anything else at all with pretensions to real flashing speed. These craft pull the wind ahead and increase its apparent strength on many headings so that they are, to all intents and purposes, going to windward when their more sedate brethren are still ambling along on uneventful reaches.

Fig 51 shows this in diagrammatic form. It is assumed that a vessel is sailing along in an 18 knot breeze blowing from just forward of the beam. If she was making 6 knots the apparent wind would be from slightly more ahead and would be blowing at what appeared to be 20.5 knots. If she could pick up her skirts still further and manage 15 knots in this breeze, the apparent wind would have drawn even further ahead at a speed of 26.5 knots. Increase velocity to 20 knots and the now 30.25 knot apparent wind will be coming from about 45 degrees off the bow. So some specialised craft can actually sail faster than the true wind speed and by bringing the breeze ahead spend a lot of their sailing life effectively going to windward. On these boats an aspect-ratio of up to 7 is appropriate. More generally a ratio of 5 to 5.5 on Bermudian rigs is a happy compromise between the conflicting demands of efficiency and reasonably priced rigs where masts can be simply stayed.

If the reader is designing a boat purely for his (or her) own enjoyment without a thought for commercial success where

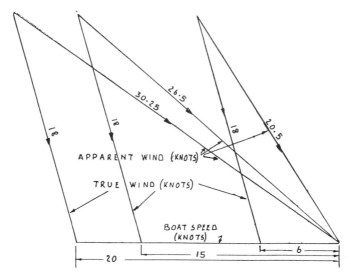

Fig 51 The faster a boat can sail in relation to wind speed the more she will bring the wind ahead.

custom and convention rule the day, do not be afraid to experiment with the rig. As long as the hull is of fairly normal form and the lead of the centre of effort over the centre of lateral resistance suggested in Chapter 3 is vaguely adhered to, even the oddest of rigs should produce some reasonable results. And there is one avenue still worth exploring. Twist in a sail where the top sags off to leeward compared with its well controlled bottom (set on a boom or similar), reduces its efficiency considerably. Such twist, though not generally too bad, is difficult to overcome on a Bermudian sail. On a gaff sail, though, twist is commonly much worse, which accounts in part for its inferior performance to windward, but is easier, theoretically, to control. A vang from the peak of the main gaff to the mizzen masthead might do the trick with an alternative of vangs port and starboard down to the yacht's quarters. If this twist could be eliminated entirely, gaff and lugsail rigs could well be more efficient than Bermudian, even to windward.

Having considered one aspect of hull form and prismatic coefficient, with a foray into sail plans, we might now shift our attention back to hulls and their reaction to the heeling forces applied by sails.

Hull balance

In Chapter 3, recommendations were made for the 'lead' of the centre of effort (CE) over the centre of lateral resistance (CLR). This put the CE a certain distance ahead of the CLR, which is correct in practice. But if the boat pivots about her CLR and the drive of the sails is through the CE, putting the CE ahead of the CLR should produce a most undesirable lee helm with the bow constantly falling off the wind (Fig 52) and only dousing the headsail, say, would allow the much preferable weather helm.

In practice, then, the CLR must shift forward of its assumed, theoretical position until it is ahead of the CE. This happens automatically on the vast majority of boats because of build-up of water pressure near the lee bow when driving along under sail. The phenomenon may be exaggerated on very bluff-bowed craft where the usual lead of CE over CLR can usefully be increased by way of compensation.

A boat is safer, comes about faster, and has superior windward ability with a small amount of weather helm (where the bow wants to come up into the wind). It is safer because in an emergency with the tiller or wheel abandoned the yacht will swing up into the wind and stop. She will come about faster because her natural inclination is to start the manoeuvre which only has to be completed with crew participation; and her better performance can be explained as follows. Assume that the weather side is to starboard. Weather helm means that the rudder blade is over to port, as in Fig 52, keeping the boat on a straight course and dissuading the bow from swinging into the wind. Water pressure on the inclined blade will create a sideways drift to starboard which resists leeway.

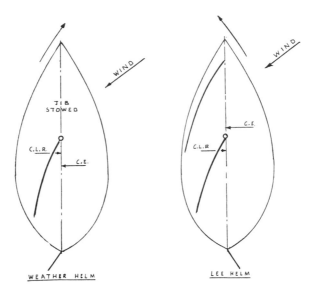

Fig 52 In practice, despite the contrary positioning when planning a sail layout, the centre of effort (CE) must lie aft of the CLR or lee helm would result.

As a yacht heels, she normally puts quite buoyant stern quarters into the water which are ill-matched by the comparatively lean bow. The result is that the vessel trims down by the head and surges up into the wind. On some craft, with exaggerated differences in form between bow and stern, the resulting bows-down attitude is fairly drastic with almost uncontrollable weather helm. The rudder may even be raised so high by this action that it becomes more or less useless in controlling the situation. This is obviously not to be recommended and the likelihood of its happening can be estimated by carrying out what is called a Rayner analysis.

On the sections of the craft are drawn heeled waterlines inclined at, perhaps, 15 degrees as in Fig 53. Here it has been done for both the round bilge and hard chine versions of the 20 ft day sailer (Figs 22 and 33). The areas of the immersed

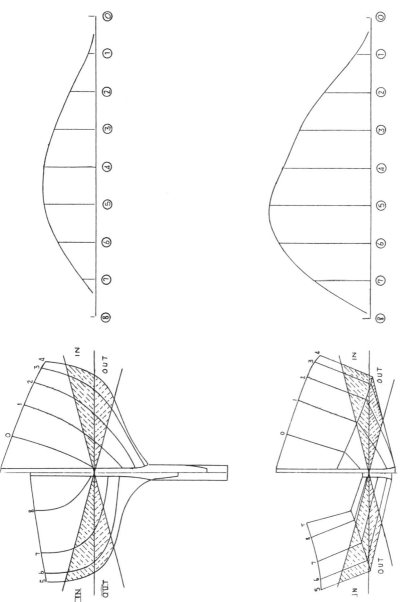

Fig 53 A Rayner analysis for hull balance carried out on both the hard chine and round bilge versions of the 20 ft day sailer.

103

('in') and emerged ('out') wedges are measured for each section. The figures for station 5 are, just as an example, 1.93 sq ft and 0.825 sq ft, respectively, on the chine version and 1.74 sq ft ('in') and 1.22 sq ft ('out') for the round bilge type. The areas of the 'out' wedges are then subtracted from those of the 'in' wedges and those answers plotted at some suitable scale out from a base line. Thus on the chine boat the point on station 5 will be $1.93 - 0825 = 1.105$ out from the base. And so on. A curve is drawn through all the points thus given and the result studied for excesses of area aft of the midships station. Most vessels will show some greater area aft and the greater this imbalance, the more uninhibited will be the surges up to windward.

It will be seen that in our examples, the round bilge double-ender shows little difference in those areas forward and aft of midships. Therefore the boat is likely to be well balanced and easy on the helm. The chine type, on the other hand, has a considerable excess of area aft and will probably have a fair amount of weather helm, especially when well heeled over. The excess of 'in' wedge area is concentrated around station 5, not far aft of midships. If it had been still further aft the tendency to drive up to windward would increase.

A glance at the two sets of sections will demonstrate what has to be done to bring the chine type nearer to the round bilge standard of balance, but do not labour too hard to achieve what, on paper, might appear to be a perfectly balanced hull. Some weather helm is desirable while, occasionally, factors come into play affecting balance which do not show up in drawing or calculation. Practically, in the last resort with a hideously unbalanced hull, vastly increasing the size of the rudder may prove a solution. Not only does this give the helmsman greater leverage to control the boat's antics but it brings the CLR further aft which is generally desirable in such cases.

Aspect-ratio of hull appendages

Especially for windward work 'lift' from keel, centreboard and even the rudder are important factors for good performance and the more lift the better. So for this element of sailing it is worth taking advantage of the fact that area for area these hull appendages are most efficient if they have a high aspect-ratio, which in this case is depth^2/area.

The limiting factor is practicality. Though it would be nice to have a centreboard, say, with an aspect-ratio of 6, such a structure is rather prone to damage. On a craft intended for deep water operation damage may be unlikely and a high aspect board drawn with a clear conscience.

Fins, rudders, centreboards and even bilge keels ideally should have a thickness of about 12–15 per cent of their fore and aft length and this maximum width should be about 30 per cent of the length from the nose.

End plates

Basically, end plates are flat bars fitted to but wider than the bottom faces of keels, the top and bottom faces of rudders and so on. They help stop water leaking over from the high pressure to the low pressure side of the structure, causing loss of lift. The famous wing keel on the Australian America's Cup winner was an end plate, amongst other things. Its shape also made it possible to use it as ballast with weight thus concentrated very low down. End plates on keels are rather vulnerable on boats that take the ground.

Propellers on sailing craft

In Chapter 4 some general guidance on propeller diameters was given which can be summed up as that it always pays (from the standpoint of harnessing power efficiently) to use the largest and slowest turning propeller that can be managed. To some extent this dictum is modified to take the speed of the vessel into account and this was covered. However, propellers on sailing vessels are something of a special case, for dragging along a large propeller, designed purely for propulsive efficiency, may cause an unacceptable loss in performance when under sail.

This is a dilemma. To fit a propeller which is too small may mean that in an emergency (just when efficiently harnessed power is needed most) the propeller may be doing little other than beating the water into a froth. Probably the most acceptable solution is to select a propeller diameter that suits the engine fitted with a direct drive gearbox; forget reduction gears. The loss in sailing speed caused by dragging the propeller around may then be around 5 per cent. This drop compares unhappily with the 0.1 drop that might be expected with a folding, centre-line prop. But unless you are quite sure that the engine will never be needed other than for calm water manoeuvring, accept the inevitable.

In round terms, a three-blade propeller is better at pushing a comparatively heavy yacht (heavy, mainly because of its ballast keel) than a two-bladed propeller but the latter causes less drag; a centreline installation is less of an impediment than a wing installation; and a folding type slightly less than a feathering propeller. Unless an exceptionally free-turning shaft/gearbox can be arranged allowing the shaft to freewheel at over about 100 rpm it is generally better to use a shaft brake under sail for reduced drag.

6 Constructional considerations

There are many ways of building a boat, ranging from traditional timber construction in one of its many forms (carvel, clinker and double diagonal amongst them) to its modern derivatives such as cold moulding and strip planking. Then there is ply and, of course, steel and aluminium alloy. Glassfibre (GRP), though probably uneconomic for a 'one-off', is to be seen everywhere and some of its virtues may be translated into foam sandwich construction (GRP skins with a foam core between); this is quite often used on individual boatbuilding projects. Ferro-cement may also be considered where weight does not matter too much and where limited funds are available for hull construction.

Each method of building has its merits and drawbacks which interest a designer and which influence his final choice of material. There will be a brief discussion of such matters in this section. First, though, a few thoughts on the general subject of the likely final weight of the hull. A crude but reasonably effective guide is to work out a skin thickness based on the thickness of a successful example in another material; not forgetting to add in the weight of suitable framing and stiffening as suggested in Chapters 2 and 3.

Suppose, then, that we have gathered from some source that 12 mm ply would be a good skinning material but the designer wants to investigate the possibilities of aluminium alloy and GRP. How thick must each be and how much would it weigh? Use the formula:

$$\text{Thickness}_A = \text{Thickness}_B \times \sqrt[3]{\frac{\text{Modulus}_B}{\text{Modulus}_A}}$$

This raises the question, what is 'modulus'? In fact it is Young's Modulus of elasticity (E) or tensile modulus and a measure of stiffness. Table 3 gave the weight of steel, aluminium alloy, ply, timber and so forth. Parts of this are repeated in Table 15 and extended to suggest the relevant E, or Young's modulus.

So, going back to the formula just given, let us put it to a practical test by assuming that we want to work out a skin thickness equivalent in stiffness to that 12 mm ply. We want figures for aluminium alloy and GRP, with aluminium first:

$$\text{Thickness aluminium} = \text{thickness ply} \times \sqrt[3]{\frac{\text{Modulus ply}}{\text{Modulus aluminium}}}$$

Table 15 Weight and modulus of elasticity of various boatbuilding materials. Normal hardwood planking will have figures quite close to ply's

Material	Weight lb/sq ft/mm (kg/m²/mm)	Young's Modulus 10^6 lbf/in² (10^3/kgf/mm)
Steel	1.6 (7.8)	30 (21)
Aluminium alloy	0.56 (1.73)	10 (7)
GRP	0.3 (1.46)	1.3–1.6 depending on type of laminate (0.9–1.1)
Marine ply	0.14 (0.68)	1.8 (1.2)

Putting in figures:

$$\text{Thickness aluminium} = 12 \times \sqrt[3]{\frac{1.8}{10}}$$

Thickness aluminium $= 12 \times 0.56$

Aluminium thickness $= 6.72$ mm, or 7 mm near enough.

In Table 15 it will be seen that aluminium alloy weighs 0.56 lb/sq ft/mm thick. So 7 mm plate will weigh 3.92 lb/sq ft.

For the same stiffness 12 mm ply at 0.14 lb/sq ft/mm thick will be 12×0.14, or 1.68 lb/sq ft. A clear theoretical victory for ply.

The same sort of sum for 2:1 resin/glass ratio, all-chopped strand mat GRP laminate would go:

$$\text{Thickness GRP} = 12 \times \sqrt[3]{\frac{1.8}{1.3}}$$

Thickness GRP $= 13.37$ mm. Say, 14 mm.

Glassfibre with a 2:1 resin/glass ratio weighs 0.3 lb/sq ft/mm so that a 14 mm thick laminate will weigh 14×0.3 lb/sq ft. That is 4.2 lb/sq ft, so proving to be heavier than either the ply or aluminium, in theory.

Just to clear one thing up when dealing with GRP, weight is usually specified as the weight of glassfibre reinforcement in the laminate only. Thus, a 4 oz laminate has 4 oz/sq ft of glass in it. These days a resin/glass ratio of 2:1 is quite common which means that the 4 oz lay-up will also have 2×4, or 8 oz of laminating resin per square foot. This laminate will then actually weigh 12 oz/sq ft but the weight tables in this book have already taken that into consideration.

Just to summarise things so far, Table 16 shows the relative stiffness of rival boatbuilding materials and associated weights. As has been inferred, though, there is more to selecting skin thickness than simply working out relative stiffnesses. Ply, for instance, is not very effective when it comes to impact resistance. Some tests done on different materials showed that with an

Table 16 Actual and relative weights of materials compared with 12 mm marine ply. As in Table 15, hardwoods will be quite close to ply, but some timbers such as fir and ash are likely to be lighter. All figures are based on equivalent stiffness

Material	Weight lb/sq ft (kg/m²)	Relative weight
Steel	7.52 (3.4)	1.00
Aluminium alloy	3.92 (1.76)	0.52
GRP	4.21 (1.89)	0.54
Marine ply	1.68 (0.74)	0.21

impact energy of 9 ft/lb, 18 swg (standard wire gauge) mild steel (2 lb/sq ft) was dented; 14 swg aluminium alloy (1.1 lb/sq ft) was also dented and the panel bent; 6 mm plywood at 0.8 lb/sq ft suffered a fracture of all plies; while two layers of $1\frac{1}{2}$ oz chopped strand mat glassfibre with a 2:1 resin/glass ratio (0.56 lb/sq ft) got away with only slight crazing.

There is a lesson there somewhere which might be that enthusiasm should be tempered by discretion. Stiffness is a good guide but not the only one. Table 16a shows an American study done on a 30 ft, shallow-bodied, fin-keel yacht, 24 ft on the waterline with 10 ft 6 in beam and 5 ft 6 in draught (9.1 m × 7.3 m × 3.2 m × 1.7 m) to determine hull weight, including framing, gave the following results which tend to confirm our league table of comparative weights based on equal stiffness, though with not quite the dramatic differences we managed.

The study did not include steel which would have been the heaviest, or conventional timber building (whose weight would have come out fairly close to steel) while our league table of relative stiffness left out both foam sandwich and traditional construction, there being too many variables in both for them to be useful in such a table.

Now for a brief look at the rival forms of building, beginning with ply.

Table 16a American comparative study on a 30 ft, shallow-bodied, fin-keel yacht (24 ft on waterline, 10.6 in beam, 5 ft 6 in draught)

Material	Construction weight
Aluminium alloy	735 lb (333 kg)
Solid GRP	976 lb (442 kg)
GRP foam core	652 lb (295 kg)
Ply	486 lb (220 kg)
Cold moulded	606 lb (274 kg)

Ply construction

Rather sadly, ply seems to be associated with the cheap and nasty end of the market. Yet good quality marine plywood has been available for many years and, if used properly, has proved to have a long life. There are probably two reasons for its bad reputation. The first is that there has been a flood of poor quality imports claiming to be marine ply and even stamped BS 1088 yet with the core material resembling nothing more than blotting paper. When attacked with a saw, great voids are revealed and considerable areas which are totally bereft of glue. No wonder it has a short life when used as a structural material on a boat.

Marine ply should indeed be to BS 1088 but this has strict rules about the core veneers, which must be virtually to the same specification as the face veneers and both have to be of one of a number of specified tropical hardwoods. Lloyds, in their guidance on the selection of timbers for use as marine plywood, class Agba, Guarea, Idigbo and Utile as being 'durable' while Makore is classed as 'very durable'.

The glue used has to be BS 1203 WBP (weather and boil proof) which makes joints highly resistant to weather, micro-organisms, cold and boiling water, steam and dry heat. The glue used is a phenolic resin. Marine ply produced in this country to BS 1088 is 'kite marked' which implies that it has been inspected during manufacture. Failing this guarantee of quality, ply should be bought that either has an undertaking as to its performance or is personally recommended by someone who knows what he is talking about.

Plywood produced in this country can be obtained in long lengths (up to 30 ft or more) which is often useful. The 4 ft (1220 mm) wide boards are scarphed together at the makers to the length required and these joints, being machine made, are likely to be of a higher standard than those constructed on the workbench.

The second reason for the unpopularity of plywood and its often short life is that not enough attention has been paid to preventing water creeping into exposed raw edges and eventually causing delamination. To some extent this was due to bad design but equally there were no easily available and simple to use materials suitable for the cure. Today, though, the epoxies in their various forms make a very effective water barrier if brushed on exposed edges and used as fillers to work into less than perfect joints.

Epoxies, too, can be used in conjunction with lightweight filler material such as microballoons to form joints. An example would be where they replace the traditional timber chine piece.

Fig 54 shows the midship section of a 15 ft 2 in by 3 ft 6 in (4.6 m × 1.1 m) rowing/sailing skiff (Figs 55 and 56). Here a simple ply construction is used with light battens at chines and deck, more to give a fair edge to the plywood panels than for structural reasons. These edge connections are backed up with glassfibre tape and epoxy resin on the outside of the joint for strength and watertightness. The battens would be glued to the frames, with a gap-filling epoxy mix in the joint opening.

Fig 57 attempts to relate timber planking thickness in inches to the boat's displacement in cubic feet. Remember that a cubic foot of sea water weighs 64 lb and that there are 35 cu ft of sea water to the ton. So if you know the displacement of a boat in pounds or tons you also know its displacement in cubic feet.

Planking thickness may be reduced by about 25 per cent for ply or cold moulded construction.

The dotted lines give an example. Assumed is a boat with 125 cu ft (3.57 tons) displacement. The cube root of 125 is 5.

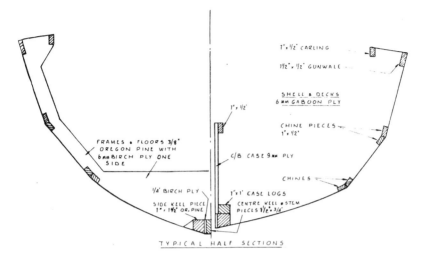

Fig 54   The midship section of a rowing/sailing skiff where epoxy resin and glass tape are used to waterproof and strengthen.

This gives a planking thickness of just over 3/4 in (19 mm) or just over 1/2 in (12 mm) in ply or cold-moulded construction. This thickness is in association with frames at 12 in (300 mm) spacing and which, in this case, have a sectional area of about 2 sq in (1290 mm^2). That means the frames could be something like $1\frac{3}{4}$ in $\times 1\frac{1}{4}$ in (45 mm $\times$ 32 mm) but if the frame spacing is changed, the planking thickness should be changed in proportion. Note that frame area is based on the square root, not cube root of the volumetric displacement.

Cold moulding

Sheet plywood construction is used almost exclusively with hard chine forms. The frames are commonly extended down to the floor (the boat being built upside-down) and the ply panels

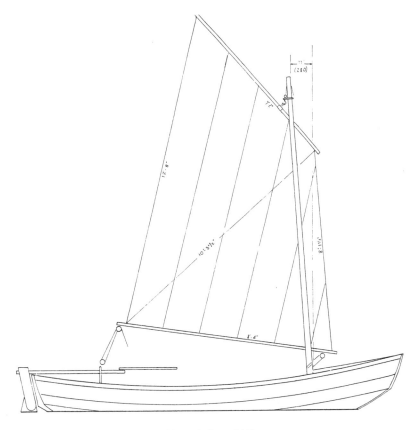

Fig 55   Above water profile of the skiff.

fastened direct to the frames, chine, beam shelf, keel and so on, which are let into those frames.

With cold moulding, temporary frames are set up and clad in closely spaced battens, to form a batten mould. Into this are generally let the keel, stem and, possibly, stern post. The planking is then fastened to the battens, keel and stem; the first, inside layer being isolated from the battens with thin plastic sheet to prevent everything sticking together. There are a minimum of three skins – the first two running diagonally in

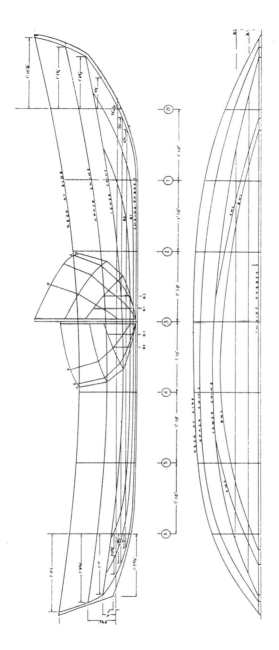

Fig 56 Lines plan of the rowing/sailing skiff.

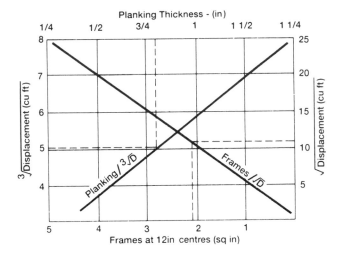

Fig 57 Plank thickness and area of stiffener or frame cross section plotted against the cube root or square root of displacement volume. The figures obtained apply to normal carvel planking but can be modified to suit other planking methods as suggested in the text.

opposite directions with the outside skin lying either fore and aft or diagonally again in the same direction as the first layer. The skins, which may be of ply or veneer strips, are glued together on the mould and when this is done the hull is lifted off the mould complete with keel, stem and so forth, for the frames and bulkheads to be fitted.

Figs 58 and 59 show a profile and lines plan for a 24 ft × 8 ft (7.3 m × 2.4 m) low speed fishing cruiser with a 3/4 in (19 mm) cold moulded hull. An extension of the cold moulding process allows frameless construction to be used if it is considered necessary. What happens is that the hull is first strip-planked over the mould. Strip planks are fairly narrow, run fore and aft and are edge glued. On this structure normal cold moulding is done, glued to the strip planking. This results in a hull at least 7/8 in (22 mm) thick and probably weighing a bit over

116

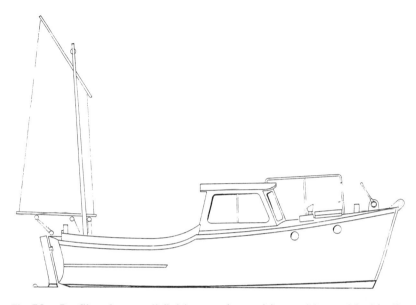

Fig 58   Profile of a small fishing cruiser with a cold-moulded hull.

2 lb/sq ft. Thus it may not be suitable for boats much below 30 ft (9.1 m) in length while it is somewhat labour intensive. Still, a nice uncluttered inside hull surface is something worth taking trouble over. Cold moulding produces a strong, light hull. Like all glued structures it is not easy to repair and having to make a batten mould first is a nuisance.

WEST ™

The letters stand for 'wood epoxy saturation technique', which is misleading since the epoxy resin that is used encapsulates the timber rather than saturates it. The Gougeon brothers in the USA first developed epoxy resins that would seal wood very effectively and made splendid gap-filling glues. Other companies have also now produced resins to do the same job.

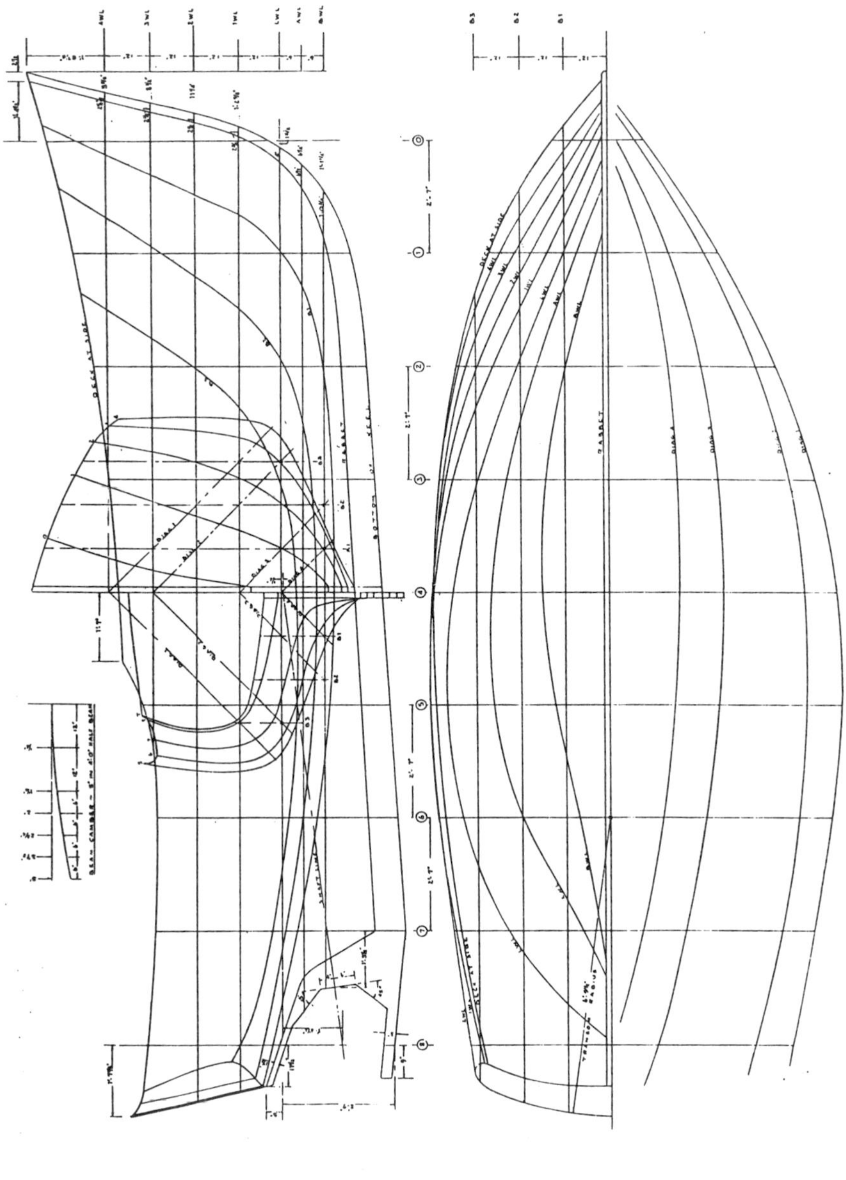

Fig 59   Lines plan of the low speed fishing cruiser.

Timbers such as fir, ash, spruce and cedar have potential strength/weight ratios considerably higher than any rival boat-building materials, with the possible exception of some of the 'exotics' used in conjunction with foam/sandwich construction (see the section on GRP, page 129). For this potential to be realised the wood must have a low moisture content and this can be achieved by first artificially drying the timber to a moisture content of, say, 12 per cent, and then coating it with one of these epoxy resins. Modern paints are good at repelling water but not so effective against water vapour (which is a gas).

The whole structure of the yacht must be thoroughly epoxy-coated inside and out, leaving no bare patches of the type that would occur between frames and planking on a traditionally built vessel. Because greater care can be exercised in ensuring close fitting joints (epoxy glued joints, of course) the WEST™ system is most commonly found in association with cold moulding.

As the moisture content is low and kept low, the timber does not shrink and swell with every change in the weather (at least not to the same extent as untreated wood) and the chances of rot developing are small.

Traditional timber (with variations)

Cold moulding and ply construction is almost always done with the hull built upside down for ease of working. On conventional construction, though, the boat is more usually worked on right way up; it all depends on the whim of the builder.

With clinker planking where the planks overlap and are fastened together with copper nails and roves (a rove is a kind of washer through which the nail passes and is then cut to the right length and flattened over the rove to form a sort of rivet) the boat's backbone of stem, keel, transom and so forth is set up first together with the building patterns or moulds which define the correct shape. The planking is then done and only now are the frames put in. These are usually timbers of quite small section which, after steaming, are supple enough to be bent into position. They are fastened to the planking with more copper nails and roves. Building moulds are then removed and can be used again if required.

Clinker planking can be about 10 per cent thinner than conventional carvel planking. The resultant boat is thus lighter but because it uses, normally, only small, steamed timbers rather than conventional frames is most suited to vessels under about 30 ft (9.1 m) in length. Minor repairs are straightforward since there are no glued joints but major work demands expert attention. Maintenance tends to be time-consuming, mainly because the interior has many timbers crossing overlapping planking, leaving voids behind which are difficult to clean, let alone paint.

Carvel planking has the individual planks lying flush with each other, the gap between them being filled with caulking cotton and white lead putty (or, today, a synthetic caulking compound). The hull may be framed with steamed timbers as in clinker building or with frames cut or laminated to shape. Very occasionally steel frames are used, in which case the whole thing is known as composite construction.

If sawn or laminated frames are used they are set in place and connected to the keel via their floors before planking starts. In other words the frames take the place of the building moulds but, unlike moulds, are a part of the permanent structure. A traditionally built carvel boat is quite heavy, in weight somewhere between GRP and steel. As with clinker boats minor repairs are quite simple; major work, less so. If carefully built of good materials and subsequently well maintained these traditionally constructed craft have a long life expectancy.

Double diagonal

One variation in planking methods that has a long and honourable history uses double diagonal planking, as demonstrated on all the previous generations of RNLI lifeboats and many of the Second World War torpedo boats. Like clinker work it can be reduced in thickness by about 10 per cent compared with the carvel planking recommendations set out in Fig 57.

As with cold moulded construction the first two layers of planking lie diagonally but in opposite directions. Cold moulding goes on to add a third skin but double diagonal stops at two, and rather than being glued together the layers are fastened together with copper nails and roves with the planking sandwiching a layer of unbleached calico soaked in white lead paint. This must still be wet when the planks are riveted together. The calico covers the gaps which occur at each plank crossing. Steamed timbers are normally employed to give a strong, flexible hull which uses, advantageously, comparatively short lengths of planking. Repairs tend to be difficult and eventually when the calico/white lead paint dries out this waterproofing layer may start to leak; such leaks are very difficult to cure.

Strip and long diagonal planking

These are both schemes where the plank edges are glued together with the result that, though they are strong, they are also difficult to repair. With strip planking, quite narrow planks run fore and aft. Edges may be bevelled to give a close fit or one edge on each plank is rounded, the other hollowed, thus allowing one to sit in the other, eliminating the need for bevelling on most planks. This rounding and hollowing would be done by woodworking machinery, not by hand on the bench. Especially where strip planking round a tight turn, fastenings are used down through the planks to pull them together. These may be nails, or wood dowels about 1/8 in diameter.

As an alternative to bevelling or rounding, square edge planks may be used, keeping the edges tight on the inside and subsequently filling the resultant gap on the outside with a low density epoxy filler.

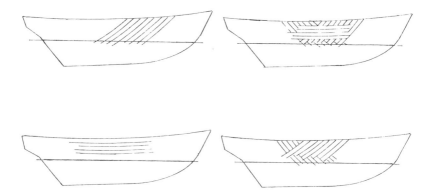

Fig 60   The run of planking in different building methods. Going clockwise from the top, left-hand sketch are: long diagonal; triple skin cold moulding; double diagonal; and strip planking.

Long diagonal planking employs a single skin, running diagonally (Fig 60). Basically the method of working is to butt succeeding planks against one another; run a spindle up the jointing faces to cut away the wood for a perfect fit; then push one plank against the other and glue the edges. Like double diagonal work, this system needs only comparatively short lengths of planking. Again planks can be through fastened in awkward areas.

Steel

Steel is undeniably heavy and in thicknesses below $\frac{1}{8}$ in (3 mm) is very prone to distortion when welding. Since 3 mm plate weighs some 5 lb/sq ft (24.5 kg/m^2) it will not be much use for any boat under about 25 ft (7.6 m) in length. Yet it is strong and stiff; if your steel-hulled cruiser was to be carried on to a coral reef, it might buckle and distort but it is likely to remain watertight when other materials have shattered. It is also fairly easy to effect temporary repairs by welding on a patch. If built under cover using shot-blasted and primed steel it will have a long, low-maintenance life. Further blasting can be done on damaged and welded areas before final priming with any of the excellent coatings available today – epoxies amongst them. If built in the open, then shot blasting should be done to the bare steel at the last stage and should be primed as quickly as possible (within a few hours). Pre-primed steel is not then particularly useful as it tends to deteriorate in the weather and show unwelcome rusty patches. So the whole boat, inside and out, will need shot blasting anyway.

The fact that it is difficult to use steel of thicknesses under 3 mm has been mentioned and this can lead to problems on small yachts and motor sailers with extensive steel superstructures, wheelhouses and the like. Normally in boatbuilding, the designer tries to arrange things so that the higher above the waterline a structure is, the thinner or lighter are the materials used. This, of course, is to aid stability (more on this in Chapter 7) by keeping the vertical centre of gravity (vcg) as low as possible. But if one is stuck with 3 mm steel there is not much that can be achieved in that direction. On these craft, then, it is often sensible to consider superstructures in ply or aluminium alloy.

To do this, a steel flat bar is welded round the periphery of the upperworks, inclined in from the vertical by an amount to match the tumblehome of the superstructure. To this is bolted the ply and its timber stiffeners.

In the case of aluminium, there should be an insulating tape between the steel bar and aluminium plate. Bolts can be galvanised steel or stainless steel. If made of stainless steel, they should be fitted through sleeves of an inert material, like nylon, with inert washers under the heads and nuts. This is to prevent electrolytic action between the steel and alloy which would eat away the aluminium.

Table 17 shows the galvanic series with the noble or cathodic metals at the top. They will tend to attack the base or anodic metals towards the bottom and the further apart they are in the table the more vicious will be the action in sea water. Stainless steel appears twice. This is because it normally forms

Table 17 The galvanic series. Those at the noble end will attack those at the base end when in close proximity in sea water

Noble or cathodic end	
Stainless steel type 316	Lead
Stainless steel type 304	Stainless steel with oxide destroyed
Stainless steel type 321	Cast iron
Monel	Mild steel
Gunmetal	Aluminium alloys
Phosphor bronze	Cadmium plating
Admiralty brass	Galvanised steel
Red brass	Zinc
Copper	Magnesium
Naval brass	**Base or anodic end**
Manganese bronze	

a protective film round itself (like aluminium alloy) but should that be destroyed, as might be the case, for instance, where stainless steel is used as a propeller shaft and the underwater bearing through which it passes wears off the protective film, it drops down the galvanic series towards the base end. It is obvious, incidentally, why zinc anodes are used. Practically every other metal will attack it in preference to metals which might be structurally essential. Magnesium anodes are normally used in fresh water.

Returning to steel construction, integral fuel tanks save space and money. They need big manholes in them so that inspection and maintenance can be carried out. Water tanks should be made of stainless or aluminium alloy; water is considerably more corrosive to steel than diesel fuel.

The specification of steel used in boatbuilding is usually BS 4360 43A, which is a conventional mild steel. Special steels such as Corten, which has a low carbon content but additional copper and manganese, are sometimes used but, in general, their greater cost and possible welding difficulties rule them out.

Some suggested skin thicknesses are given in the sections on timber and GRP, but thicknesses for steel have not been attempted since plate thicknesses are largely governed by what is commercially available. It would be no use, for example, working out that a craft of 5 tons displacement required 3.6 mm plating, since this specification is unavailable.

What can be said in general terms is that below 30 ft (9.1 m), 3 mm plating for bottom, sides and decks might be appropriate with something like 65 mm × 50 mm × 6 mm ($2\frac{1}{2}$ in × 2 in × $\frac{1}{4}$ in) frames at about 3 ft 3 in (1 m) centres. From 30–40 ft (9.1–12.2 m) length, 4 mm bottom and side plating might be used with 3 mm decks. Frames could be increased to 75 mm × 50 mm × 6 mm (3 in × 2 in × $\frac{1}{4}$ in) at that 3 ft 3 in spacing. Above 40 ft we are moving towards 6 mm bottom plating with 4 mm topsides and decks. Frames might now be 80 mm × 60 mm × 6 mm ($3\frac{1}{2}$ in × $2\frac{1}{2}$ in × $\frac{1}{4}$ in) on the same centres as before which fit in quite well with an accommodation bulkhead spacing of 2 m. None of these suggestions reduces the need to consult the rules of the classification societies (such as Lloyds) if the job is to be done properly. Their purpose is simply to give the designer some idea of what he is letting himself in for.

Apart from, maybe, a collision bulkhead forward, steel bulkheads are best avoided in small craft. They are heavy and tend to be wavy, needing cladding if they are to look reasonable. Ply bulkheads are generally preferable. In bigger boats there might be steel bulkheads forward and aft of the engine compartment. It is easy to make steel bulkheads watertight.

Figs 61 and 62 show the lines and list of scantlings for a 55 ft junk-rigged ketch. There is nothing of very great note except that chine bars have been used. These are not strictly necessary but some builders like them both to prevent chafing damage at what might be considered vulnerable corners if the plates were simply butted up and welded (as is quite common) and to give a fair curve to the chine. Their drawback is that twice as many welding runs have to be made than if the side and bottom plates were butted.

Welding on steel boats may be normal electric arc (versatile and economical) or by one of the shielded arc processes where the arc is shrouded in an inert gas such as CO. This latter method produces less distortion, is somewhat more expensive and rather unsuitable for building in the open where wind can disturb the shielding gas.

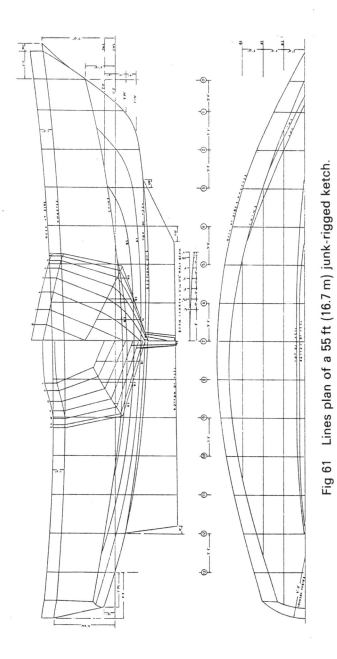

Fig 61   Lines plan of a 55 ft (16.7 m) junk-rigged ketch.

Scantlings

Bottom of keel	9 mm
Keel sides	6 mm
Bottom shell	5 mm
Side shell	5 mm
Decks and cockpit sole	4 mm
Floors	6 mm
Bulkheads	4 mm
Brackets	6 mm with 8 in arms
Face bar	65 mm ×6 mm
Gunwale bar	5 in O.D. tube
Chine bar	3 in O.D. tube or 100 × 9 F.B.
Stem bar	100 mm × 12 mm F.B.
Hull frames	130 mm ×6 mm F.B.
Deck beams	80 mm ×6 mm F.B.
Bulkhead stiffs	65 mm ×6 mm F.B.
Pillars	65 mm ×4 mm tube on alternate beams
Hull stringers	65 mm ×6 mm F.B.
Deck stringers	40 mm ×6 mm F.B.
Engine beds	6 mm

Fig 62   List of the principal steel scantlings from the same 55 ft ketch.

Aluminium alloy

Most boats are built (in much the same way as steel) of alloys such as NE5 or NE8 for extrusions, NS5 or NS8 for sheet and so on. These are weldable alloys but welding must be by a shielded arc process.

Like steel, aluminium can distort while welding and something like 3/16 in ($4\frac{1}{2}$ mm) plate is the minimum thickness that can be welded with the expectation of distortion-free completion.

Aluminium, having a Young's Modulus of 10 as compared with steel's 30×10^{6}, needs to be about 1.5 times as thick as steel for equal strength and will then weigh about half as much, so it is a very worthwhile, though somewhat expensive, boatbuilding material.

All sorts of scaremongering goes on when aluminium is discussed, often with the inference that it will simply melt away given half a chance and cannot be fitted out using normal materials. This is simply not the case. Aluminium or plastic seacocks can replace the traditional bronze types; galvanised mild steel is very close to aluminium in the galvanic series table and so can be used for keel and other bolts; a stainless steel propeller shaft is automatically isolated from any alloy structure by its bearing material; a bronze propeller can be hard chrome plated if there are any worries on that score; and so on.

In fact if steel can be considered a low maintenance material when properly prepared and coated, aluminium alloys provide a no-maintenance structure. There is no need to paint them, apart from decorative and anti-fouling considerations, as they form a protective film over the surface which will form again if destroyed locally. Effective repairs may be difficult in out-of-the-way places where the correct welding gear and alloys of the right specification are conspicuous by their absence.

Ferro-concrete

Not so long ago people turned to ferro-concrete when funds were short and ambition high for it is possible to build a largish cruiser in this material for considerably less money than any other. The work involved is grindingly hard but no special skills are needed except right at the end of the building process when the concrete has to be worked through the armature of chicken wire, tubes and rods to form a smooth, fair skin inside and out without voids or air entrapment. Still, professionals can be hired to undertake this work and since it should be completed in a day the cost is not too great.

Unhappily, the hull represents only a comparatively small part of the total cost of a boat and many unfinished yachts dot our coastline as a sad testimony to this fact. Ferro-concrete boats other than those built by one or two well known yards tend to have a low re-sale value. This is not because there is anything intrinsically wrong with the material – there isn't – but it is difficult for people to judge the quality of the workmanship after the boat has been completed. What voids lurk under that shiny exterior, perhaps leading to possible corrosion and strength problems? Indeed, does the paint conceal the fact that the reinforcing is perilously close to the surface with almost inevitable rusting and then wholesale corrosion with the concrete cracking as a result? Even a surveyor will find it hard to tell.

Ferro-concrete boats cannot rot, be attacked by worms or suffer from osmosis but they are heavy, generally weighing slightly more than a steel hull. Though sometimes additives are put in the cement mix to delay curing (important in hot weather) or to reduce water requirements, most often simple Portland cement is used with a water/cement ratio of about $0:35$ with $3\frac{1}{2}$ gallons (16 litres) of water to each 112 lb (50 kg) bag of cement. The sand/cement ratio is about $2:1$ by weight.

There are two principal methods of construction. The first is to set the hull up on the boat's frames (generally steel pipe) as in traditional timber or steel construction. Keel, stem and so forth are also pipe while all these are supplemented by numerous round bar longitudinals. Several layers of chicken wire or similar steel mesh are lashed to this framework with twists of wire, and bound together by the same method. Everything is smoothed and faired to give an accurate hull shape and the cement mix is then worked through and vibrated with mechanical vibrators to reduce air entrapment. The second building scheme is to set up a batten mould as in cold moulded construction and erect the hull on that. Though this makes for easier fairing the dangers of pockets of air being left in the concrete are increased.

The finished hull is often draped in sacking and intermittently sprayed with water for a week or so to delay curing. Finally it is painted with a good waterproofing paint, such as an epoxy.

GRP

Though glassfibre reinforced plastic (GRP) is by far the most common boatbuilding material today that does not imply that it is necessarily the best. It is simply a good all-round medium, admirably suited to limited production runs. It does not rot, though it may develop osmosis; and it does not corrode though it burns spectacularly well unless fire retardant resins are used. These tend to be expensive and do not weather as well as those commonly used.

A GRP boat is made by bonding together in a mould several layers of glassfibre with, generally, a polyester resin. The glassfibre comes in several guises, the principal of which are chopped strand mat and woven rovings. Both are made from glass heated to some 1300–1400 °C in an electric furnace and then rapidly drawn through platinum bushings to be bundled together to form a strand. The strands are next either combined to form chopped strand mat, made from 1–2 in (25–50 mm) strands held together in a random manner by a resinous binder; or woven into a plain, square pattern to become woven rovings.

Chopped strand mat is comparatively cheap and forms the basis of most boat laminates. It is simple to work the resin through successive glass layers to build up the required thickness but used alone it lacks stiffness, especially if the resin content is too high. A 3:1 resin/glass ratio could lead to an E figure as low as 0.8. On many hulls, then, chopped strand mat is combined with alternate layers of the stronger woven rovings to produce E figures of as high as 1.8. The resin/glass ratio should be around 2:1.

One has to start somewhere with not too many variables, so laminate weight recommendations are normally made on a basis of chopped strand mat alone, as is Fig 63. This works with the boat's displacement as a basis. The dotted lines plot the course for a vessel where the cube root of the displacement in cubic feet is 5 (so displacement is 5^3, or 125 cu ft). The weight of the bottom laminate would then be about 8 oz of chopped strand mat and stiffeners would be spaced at 19 in centres. If woven rovings were incorporated, Young's modulus, E, might go up from 1.3 to 1.6, whereupon the bottom laminate could be reduced by the method touched on earlier.

Conventionally, GRP boats are built by first making an exact replica of the vessel in some stable timber (this replica being

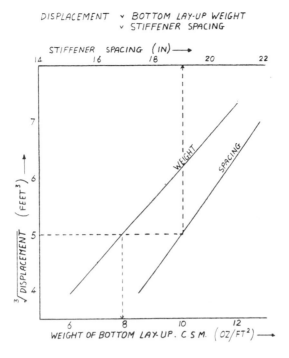

Fig 63   Suggested weight of bottom laminate (in chopped strand mat with a 2:1 resin/glass ratio) and stiffener spacing based on the cube root of the volumetric displacement.

known as the plug); then taking a mould off it; and finally laminating inside the mould. This is clearly uneconomic for a 'one-off', but a substitute constructional scheme is on offer. This is to make a batten mould first, as in cold moulding, and then to cover this in a layer of rigid-cell expanded plastic such as expanded polyurethane. The foam is temporarily fastened to the mould and sheathed in GRP. It is then lifted off and sheathed on the inside with another layer of GRP. Subsequently the inevitably rather rough finish inside and out is smoothed and faired. This represents a lot of hard work.

Constructional considerations

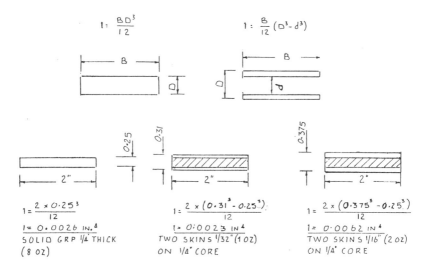

Fig 64   The method of working out the main ingredients of a foam sandwich laminate of equal strength to one of solid GRP.

Fig 64 shows how to work out the weight of laminate in foam core or sandwich building (the method described above) to equal the strength of a solid laminate. If the latter was an 8 oz lay-up (about $\frac{1}{4}$ in thick) and it was intended to use a $\frac{1}{4}$ in (6 mm) thick foam core in sandwich construction, just for the sake of argument, you would first work out the moment of inertia (I) of the solid example, taking a piece of the bottom of some arbitrary width. Here 2 in was taken but any width would do. That answer was 0.0026 in[4].

What we are aiming for is to find an I figure using the foam core and a layer of glass and resin on each side that equals, or is greater than, the figure for the solid laminate. So now we can have a go with the thinnest possible GRP lay-up of 1 oz, which is 1/32 in thick, both sides. The internal depth is still 0.25 in but outside it is now $\frac{1}{4}$ in + 1/16 in, or 0.31 in. Thus I is 0.0023 in[4], which is too low, thank goodness, for that would have been a pretty feeble affair with the outer skins too thin to resist much abrasion. Do the sum again, but this time with double the skin thickness and the answer is a satisfactory moment of inertia figure of $0.0062\,\text{in}^4$, with the hull then weighing considerably less than one of a solid laminate. Expanded foam can be taken as weighing something in the order of 4–7 lb/cu ft $(64–112\,\text{kg/m}^3)$.

The usual glass reinforcing in a laminate is E glass with an ultimate tensile strength of about 500 000 lb/sq in. In high stress areas of the hull, and to stiffen up longitudinals, even stronger reinforcing can be used, at the expense of generally more difficult 'wetting out' with the resin and inevitably higher cost. One such reinforcing is S-glass with two other better known types being carbon fibre and Kevlar. The latter is generally used in woven roving form while carbon fibre is employed mainly as a unidirectional roving to strengthen stringers and frames. It is also found in the production of unstayed masts where its stiffness is a valuable asset. Some weight is saved by using these 'exotic' reinforcings but it is impossible to generalise.

The usual unsaturated polyester laminating resin can be replaced by epoxy resin or, as a half-way house between the two, vinylester resin. Both are more expensive than the polyesters but both provide better strength, adhesion and waterproofing qualities.

7 Stability

Stability is a subject where a little knowledge is useful but more than that is unnecessary. Designers only occasionally get asked to do stability calculations, and if they are, there are learned bodies equipped with computers programmed to do the very tedious and lengthy sums. If the designer can supply the computer with the information it needs and can then understand the results produced he will have done his part.

All stability calculations revolve around knowing the positions of, first, the centre of gravity, G, and second, the centre of buoyancy, B. In past calculations we worked out the location of the longitudinal centre of gravity (lcg) by taking moments about midships. Now we could extend the process by taking moments of the same items of hull structure and equipment but this time above and below the load waterline (lwl). Divide the total moments by the total weight as before and the result would be a vertical location for G. That is the principal item of information needed by the computer but leaves unresolved a location for B.

However much a boat heels it is assumed that G remains in the same place, as indeed it will as long as nothing breaks loose and the vessel does not flood. B, though, being the centre of area of the underwater volume must shift with every different angle of heel as it moves to become the centre of the changed under-water area. The work involved in calculating this new position for many different angles of heel is lengthy, as can be imagined, and best left to the wizardry of the computer.

In all cases the weight of the vessel acts vertically down through the centre of gravity, G, while the boat's buoyancy, an equal and opposite force, acts vertically up through B. They must be equal and opposite for if B were mysteriously the greater the vessel would rise bodily in the water. If G were greater the opposite would occur.

Sketch 1 of Fig 65 shows a mythical yacht in repose. The locations of G and B are marked. Sketch 2 has the boat heeling to about 25 deg. G remains in its previous position, on the centreline and at a certain height above the keel but B has moved across to become the centre of area of the new, heeled underwater shape.

Where the vertical through B cuts the yacht's centreline is marked M, which is called the **metacentre** and the distance from G to M is the metacentric height. This is a measure of stability but a better one is the length of the righting arm, GZ. That is called the righting lever and is often used in stability diagrams, of which more will be said in a moment. If the length of the line GZ had been multiplied by the boat's displacement in tons, pounds, kilograms or what you will, the result would be termed a **righting moment**.

Returning to sketch 2, it can be seen that the opposing forces through G and B are acting to twist the boat back upright and thus are acting as what is termed a **righting couple**. It is worth noting that if G had been located at a greater height above the keel than the position shown, GM would have been less, GZ shorter and the righting couple less powerful. A boat of the same form as the one shown but with less ballast or heavier upperworks or beefier spars or, possibly, a lighter engine would have a higher G, to give a more sluggish response to heeling.

Sketches 3 and 4 follow the vessel round at increasing angles of heel (78 deg and 150 deg). In both cases M is still above G and there are still righting couples, though only just in the last

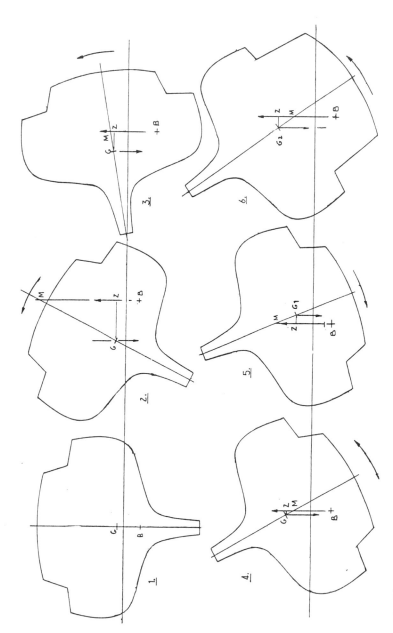

Fig 65 A yacht hull at various angles of heel showing the positions of the centres of gravity and buoyancy (G and B) in all cases.

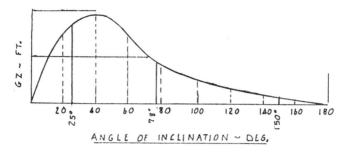

Fig 66   Curves of righting levers (GZ) plotted against angles of heel for the yacht in Fig 65.

case. If that can be sustained for a few degrees more the craft will be able to right herself from any angle of heel and would be known as a self-righter.

In Fig 66 these and other righting levers (GZ) in feet or metres are plotted against angles of keel and this is known as a **stability curve** or a curve of righting levers.

Back again to Fig 65. Sketch 5 has the boat heeled to about 150 deg as in sketch 4 but with a raised position of G, which is shown as G_1, just to demonstrate what happens when G is allowed to climb too high. Now M is below G_1 and what was a positive righting couple, GZ, has been transformed into a capsizing couple. The opposing forces through G_1 and B are acting to turn the boat well and truly upside down. This is what happens on the majority of boats; at some angle of heel the forces change sides and conspire to invert the vessel.

In sketch 6 the same hull as before has had a large superstructure added and the centre of gravity, now G_2, has risen in consequence. There is still a righting couple, however, because the vessel is floating partly on her superstructure, with B in a new and advantageous position. This is the scheme used on some RNLI lifeboats to make them self-righting. A large, watertight deckhouse does the trick but must be combined with automatically closing vents and engine intakes. So perhaps there is something to be said for capacious wheelhouses, apart from being able to take tea and biscuits out of the wind and rain. Air bags strapped to the highest point of a hull or superstructure perform the same function. On inflation they persuade the boat to float so high in the water when inverted as to become a self-righter.

It looks, then, from our efforts so far, that a low centre of gravity is a good thing and, in fact, comparing two similar vessels but with different G heights, the one with the lower G will normally have a greater maximum righting lever and will also have a greater range of stability. That is, even if not a self-righter she will still right herself from larger angles of heel.

The same applies to raising the freeboard. High freeboard, however undesirable for windage and whether caused by high topsides or high deckworks, does marvels for maximum righting moments and range of stability. That is unless G is allowed to rise too much in sympathy. Keep deckhouses and so forth as light as possible, commensurate with adequate strength.

What about beam? How does this affect things? Fig 67 is meant to bring a little light to bear. It shows the curves of

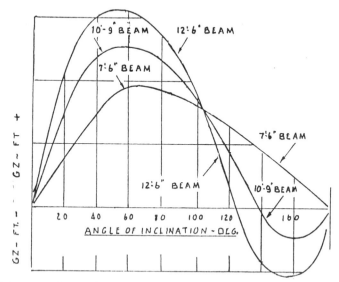

Fig 67   Three 33 ft (10 m) yachts of different beam showing the effect this has on stability. Only the narrowest is a self-righter.

righting levers for three yachts all 33 ft (10 m) in length and with 4.5 tons displacement but with beams of 12 ft 6 in (3.8 m), 10 ft 9 in (3.3 m) and 7 ft 9 in (2.4 m). Note that the curves extend below the base line for the two widest yachts. As discussed, just as there are positive righting levers trying to restore a vessel to an upright stance, there are negative righting, or capsizing levers, where the action is to invert the boat totally. That is what levers below the base are doing. It will be clear that the greater the beam the 'stiffer' the yacht will be with good righting levers initially. Thus with 12 ft 6 in beam the righting lever, GZ, at 60 degrees heel is over 3 ft; with 10 ft 9 in beam this has dropped to some 2 ft 6 in; and at 7 ft 9 in beam it is less than 2 ft. This is what we would expect, but look at the capsizing angles where GZ becomes negative and is working to capsize the vessel. The widest beam boat will capsize if heeled to angles over about 125 degrees and so will the 10 ft 9 in beam yacht at angles over, roughly, 140 deg, while the narrowest craft will have a positive, restoring lever at all angles of heel. G is assumed to be at the same height on all models.

This is the normal pattern of events. All other things being equal, a beamy boat will be stiffer than a comparable narrow rival and better able to stand up to a press of sail without excessive heel. But in the last analysis and a total knock-down the slimmer vessel is likely to right herself whereas the beamier craft may remain capsized and upside-down.

All stability calculations assume that the hull and superstructure remain watertight at all times and angles of heel. The odd dribble of water past hatchboards or through a not-quite-closed vent won't upset things unduly but an open hatch or door will most probably ensure that any potential the yacht had for self-righting is destroyed.

8 Further design considerations

Finally, some rather random thoughts on subjects which cannot really be classed as boat designing but which come into the reckoning when pursuing that activity. Accommodation, for instance; if drawing out a cruising boat it is a little disappointing, to say the least, to discover late on in the proceedings that the hoped-for layout simply won't fit in the otherwise splendid hull that reposes on the drawing board.

Accommodation

Ideas should be sketched out on the first rough lines plan just to check that all is potentially well. Think also about the siting of principal bulkheads at this stage. They should fall either well clear of frames – otherwise it may prove difficult to fit them – or on a frame which they can replace or be attached to; the latter being common practice on steel and aluminium alloy construction when ply bulkheads are used.

The first act in planning a layout is to draw the cabin sole line on the lines plan at what appears a sensible height. From this a cabin sole width can be found, bearing in mind that such things as frames can encroach quite significantly on apparently available space. Following on from the sole, sketch in bunk and work-top heights and widths, again thinking of frames.

If things get too difficult the sole can be swept up towards the bow to take advantage of the fact that the higher the sole is, the wider it will be, and that the deck is probably sweeping up also, so that no headroom is lost. This curved-in-profile sole is preferable to having steps, over which people will trip at sea. The sole can also be mildly concave in section to allow more headroom over its lowest point.

Work tops should be about 3 ft (0.9 m) above the sole and berths can be as little as 2 ft (0.6 m) wide at the shoulders tapering to 1 ft 6 in (0.45 m) at the foot. For adults they should be at least 6 ft 6 in (2 m) long. Where there are upper and lower bunks or in the case of quarter berths there should be not less than 1 ft 9 in (0.53 m) turning-over room above the mattress. Two feet (0.6 m) of clear passage is needed between obstructions such as work surfaces, lockers and bulkheads. Study chandlers' catalogues for sizes of cookers, sinks, toilets, handbasins and so forth and avoid the common pitfall of siting handbasins under side decks. Admittedly they take up little room there, which is just as well since they are also quite useless.

Fig 68 shows some sitting heights at various angles of inclination. Thus if one is almost recumbent you can get away with only about 3 ft 2 in (0.96 m) headroom under the deck, but if using a table for eating, more like 4 ft 8 in (1.42 m) is needed. The third sketch shows another possibility; note that the height to the top of the settee cushion and the slope of the backrest have to be different for each selection.

Obviously the best way to study accommodation layouts is have a look at existing boats or, failing that, to peruse the accommodation plans that frequently appear in the boating journals. As a general rule, try not to be too ambitious. A simple, uncluttered accommodation is generally to be preferred to the fussy and crowded.

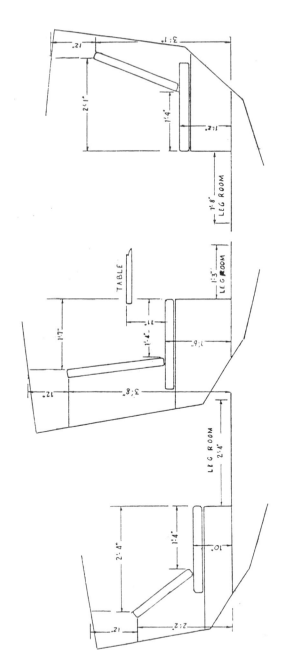

Fig 68 Minimum sitting headroom is governed by the height of the settee above the sole and the angle of its backrest.

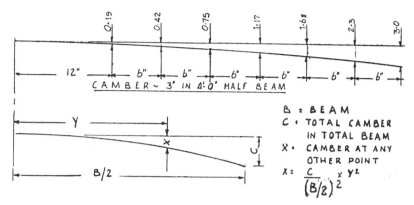

Fig 69   One way to draw a camber curve. Note that B in the formula is total, not half, beam.

Camber

Decks and cabin tops must have some curve in them, in section, both to shed water and add strength. A typical camber curve is shown in Fig 69 plus the way to draw it. The camber shown, 3 in in 4 ft half beam, is what you should aim for on decks. Cabin tops which are infrequently walked on can have a much steeper curve to aid headroom below.

Stanchions and bulwarks

For peace of mind at sea, bulwarks come high on the list of priorities. They can be as low as 1 ft (0.3 m) and still be very effective solid water and human barriers. At the same time they allow stanchions to be much more securely fastened than is normally possible on GRP and timber boats. With steel and alloy vessels, of course, stanchions can be welded directly to the deck which would have to tear up before the stanchions gave way.

Bulwarks

Bulwarks must not be allowed to hold water on deck; so they need openings cut in them. Lloyds give the following formula for the area of opening in m^2 per side. This applies to deck scuppers, scupper pipes and cockpit drains, assuming that the bulwarks form a well, as a cockpit does:

$$A = 0.01 \times 1 \times h + 0.035 \times 1 \times h^2$$

where A is the area of opening per side in m^2; l is the length of the bulkwark (or cockpit) in metres; h is the height of the bulwark (or depth of cockpit) in metres. So if a bulwark was, say, 9 m long and its depth was 0.5 m, the required area of deck scupper per side would be:

$$A = 0.01 \times 9 \times 0.5 + 0.035 \times 9 \times 0.5^2$$

$$= 0.045 + 0.079$$

$$= 0.124 \ m^2 \ \text{or} \ 1.33 \ \text{sq ft or} \ 191.5 \ \text{sq in}$$

This area could be arranged as a gap between the bottom of the bulwark and deck edge over its whole length or in the form of freeing ports spread along the length.

Stanchions

Stanchions may be spaced as far apart as 6 ft (1.8 m) but are better at about 4 ft (1.2 m) when they are stronger and follow the contours of the deck edge more closely. Fig 70 shows typical stanchion heights together with appropriate heights of the centre eye. A stanchion as low as 2 ft (0.6 m) is a poor affair, 2 ft 3 in (0.7 m) being really the practical minimum.

Rake of masts

All masts should rake aft for appearance's sake. On two- (or three)-masted rigs the forward mast should be the most upright,

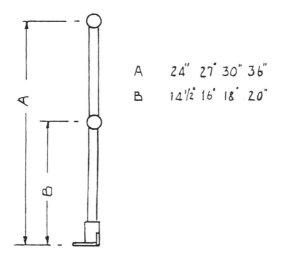

A 24" 27" 30" 36"

B 14½" 16" 18" 20"

Fig 70 Stanchions may be epoxy-painted or galvanised mild steel; aluminium alloy; or stainless steel. Don't deride mild steel. It is cheap, strong and simply fabricated.

with those further aft having successively greater rake, otherwise it appears that they are leaning in towards each other. Great rake, though looking attractive on some rigs, means that when running in light airs the booms tend to swing inboard which can be a nuisance. Single-masted rigs can rake about 1 : 35 while on ketches, yawls and the like the mainmast might have a rake of something like 1 : 25.

In conclusion

As I put together my final thoughts in this chapter, I am haunted by thoughts of 'What other aspects or further information could I have added?' But I hope that I have given the interested reader enough basic information to enable him or her to start their own projects and work through a design to the point where good performance under sail or power is reasonably assured. Further reading should fill in the finer points of detail.

Yacht design has become a rather high-tech business these days with designers using computers to aid their skills. Yet they are merely working through the same design processes as are described in this book – more swiftly and expensively but probably with no finer results than the designer crouched over a drawing board with a pad of paper and simple calculator by his side.

So if you do feel inspired to design your own boat, go ahead and give it a try. You will derive immense satisfaction and interest from the project. Just remember: be as accurate as possible with your measurements and calculations and keep your design simple.

8   Index

ADLARD COLES NAUTICAL ORDER FORM

Adlard Coles Nautical books are available through bookshops and chandlers, or can be obtained directly from A & C Black by writing to: **A & C Black, PO Box 19, Huntingdon, Cambs PE19 3SF** or telephone (01480) 212666, fax: (01480) 405014. Access and Visa are accepted. Availability and published prices are correct at the time of going to press, but are subject to change without notice.

ISBN prefix: 0–7136

Principles of Yacht Design: Lars Larsson and Rolf Eliasson 3855-9 £30
How to Choose the Right Yacht: Joachim F Muhs 3950 4 £8.99
Spray The Ultimate Cruising Boat: Bruce Roberts-Goodson 4086-3 £16.99
Complete Amateur Boatbuilding: Michael Verney 5731-6 £14.99
This is Boat Interior Construction: Michael Naujok 3612-2 £16.99
Boatowner's Mechanical and Electrical Manual 2nd edn: Nigel Calder 4291-2
Marine Electrical and Electronics Bible: John C Payne 4110-X £22.99
Boat Electrical Systems: Dag Pike 3451-0 £12.99
How to Install a New Diesel: Peter Cumberlidge 3777-3 £9.99
Surveying Small Craft 3rd edn: Ian Nicolson 3949-0 £19.99
Boat Data Book 3rd edn: Ian Nicolson 3953-9 £14.99
Fitting Out 4th edn: J D Sleightholme 3558-4 £9.99
Aluminium Boatbuilding 2nd edn: Ernest Sims 3691-2 £18.99
Surveying and Restoring Classic Boats: J C Winters 3611-1 £25
Start with a Hull: Loris Goring £14.99
Boatbuilding Techniques Illustrated: Richard Birmingham: 3642-4 £19.99
Clinker Boatbuilding: John Leather 3643-2 £12.99
Osmosis and Glassfibre Yacht Construction 2nd edn: Tony Staton-Bevan 4193-2 £12.99

Please send me the following books: _____

_____

_____

_____ I enclose a cheque for: £_____ made payable to A & C Black *(please add £1.50 for p&p)*

_____ Please debit my credit card Access/Visa ☐☐☐☐☐☐☐☐☐☐☐☐☐☐☐☐

Expiry Date: ☐☐☐☐☐

Name:_____

Address:_____

_____

☐ *I do not wish to receive information about **Adlard Coles Nautical books** in the future.*

WATCHING WILDLIFE

Tips, Gear and Great Places for Enjoying America's Wild Creatures

by

MARK DAMIAN DUDA

Illustrated by

ROBERT FIELD

FALCON™

HELENA, MONTANA

Copyright © 1995 by Falcon Press Publishing Co., Inc.
Helena and Billings, Montana.

Illustrations copyright © 1995 by Robert Field.

Printed in the United States of America.

Library of Congress Cataloging-in-Publication Data
Duda, Mark Damian.
    Watching Wildlife : tips, gear, and great places for enjoying
America's wild creatures / by Mark Damian Duda ; illustrated by
Robert Field.
       p. cm.
    ISBN 1-56044-315-4
    1. Wildlife watching—North America. 2. Wildlife watching—North
America—Equipment and supplies. I. Field, Robert. II. Title.
QL60.D84 1995
599.0973—dc20   95-26073
                                                      CIP

Front cover photo: Elf Owl, Bryan Munn
Back cover photo: Moose, Michael S. Sample

WATCHING WILDLIFE

Contents

ACKNOWLEDGMENTS

The wildlife management profession in North America is replete with dedicated biologists, educators, and administrators. Long hours and sometimes insurmountable conservation challenges never seem to dampen the dedication of these conservationists. As a result of their hard work and resourcefulness, North America has restored once depleted populations of white-tailed deer, wild turkeys, beavers, wood ducks, pronghorn antelope, Canada geese, and bald eagles. I can't imagine America without bald eagles or wood ducks, can you? For that reason, I dedicate this book to wildlife management professionals working for wildlife.

This book would not have been possible without the ideas, encouragement, enthusiasm, and patience of Falcon Press editor John Grassy. A dedicated wildlife conservationist, John helped develop many of the concepts presented here. Many other people offered invaluable assistance, materials, and information, including Bob Hernbrode of the Colorado Division of Wildlife. Much-appreciated assistance also came from Mark Hilliard, Bureau of Land Management; Cindy Swanson, USDA Forest Service; Nancy Marx, U.S. Fish and Wildlife Service; Deborah Richie, The Nature Conservancy/USDA Forest Service; Laury Marshall, Izaak Walton League; Dave McElveen, Florida Game and Fresh Water Fish Commission; Nancy Tankersley, Alaska Department of Fish and Game; and Wilderness Voyagers, Harrisonburg, Virginia. Kira Young, Cathy Thomas, and Rebecca Sipes of Responsive Management assisted in numerous ways and kept the project focused and organized.

I am especially grateful to Dr. Stephen Kellert of Yale for encouraging wildlife viewing as an activity and as a tool for teaching, and for teaching me the importance of managing the activity. Dr. Kellert urged me to take a closer look at wildlife viewing for my graduate work at Yale University in 1982, long before others recognized its significance.

I offer a special thank you for support and encouragement from my family: my wife Mary Anne, daughter Madeline, and son Mark Damian II. I am also indebted to Stanley and Barbara Duda, parents strong enough to allow their children to reach for dreams of their own.

1 | Wildlife Viewing in North America

A few years ago, after conducting a wildlife communications workshop in British Columbia, I elatedly received an invitation to go salmon fishing with Dr. Dave Narver, Director of the Ministry of the Environment's Fisheries Program. We left early the next morning, a clear, bright March day on the Strait of Juan de Fuca, the glasslike water stretching to the distant snow-covered mountains of Olympic National Park.

Lucky thing the view was spectacular. Although I was fishing with one of the best salmon fishermen around, the very director of the Fisheries Program, we went several hours without so much as a bite. (This has since become the source of many jokes.) As I pondered

8

my complete lack of angling prowess, I was startled by a large splash not fifty yards off. Another splash brought me completely out of my daydreams: a group of orcas had come upon us.

In my initial excitement I raised my arm and yelled, pointing them out to Dave—as if eighteen killer whales (each twenty-five feet long and weighing seven tons) within a stone's throw of our small boat needed pointing out. As I did so, I splashed the hot cup of coffee I was drinking all over Dave, who, until that day at least, had been an important client. What an impression I must have made.

But these were ORCAS. Their vivid black and white bodies cut the water, their large dorsal fins sliced the surface. I had always envisioned them smaller. In identification books, orcas are often pictured alongside massive blue whales or finbacks, making them appear smaller than they actually are. In the middle of the strait, viewed from a sixteen-foot runabout, they were immense.

What was most striking about the whales, however, was their sound. We were so close, so alone, and the air was so still I could hear every count of their breathing. Their massive intakes gave me a rare perspective on just how large their lungs must be. We followed them slowly for a half hour, listening and watching. Almost as quickly as they appeared, they were gone.

Wildlife viewing is one of North America's most popular and fastest-growing outdoor activities. According to National Surveys of Fishing, Hunting, and Wildlife-Associated Recreation, conducted by the U.S. Fish and Wildlife Service, the number of Americans who took trips for the specific purpose of watching wildlife increased 63 percent during the past decade. Today almost 30 million Americans take wildlife viewing trips each year. About 19 percent of Canadians take trips for the specific purpose of watching wildlife, and the Canadian Wildlife Service reports the total number of participants grew from 3.6 million to 4.4 million in the last six years, an increase of 23 percent.

We can talk about wildlife viewing in such statistical terms. But facts and figures had little to do with my morning encounter with orcas in the Strait of Juan de Fuca. On a personal level, wildlife viewing is about experiences and memories that last a lifetime. There is nothing to compare with the awe and excitement that accompany a momentary encounter with wild creatures. Despite exhaustive efforts of nature photographers, filmmakers, and writers to capture its vividness, wildlife is most fully revealed one-on-one.

WILDLIFE VIEWING AND CHILDREN

When Brian Burk of Merritt Island, Florida, was eleven years old, he spent a week at the Florida Game and Fresh Water Fish Commission's Everglades Youth Camp in West Palm Beach. There he observed deer, hawks, owls, snakes, and raccoons while at camp, and enthusiastically remarked later, "You learn more when you're outside. When you experience it, you remember it. It's better to learn about wildlife for yourself!"

Brian's experience backs up the findings of most research [see sidebar, page 14]. These show that the best way to foster positive attitudes about wildlife and the natural environment is direct participation in outdoor activities such as hiking, wildlife viewing, and bird identification.

Aldo Leopold remembered his own early experiences with wildlife. Considered by some to be the father of wildlife management in America, Leopold remarked in *A Sand County Almanac*, "My earliest impressions of wildlife and its pursuit retain a vivid sharpness of form, color and atmosphere that half a century of professional wildlife experience has failed to obliterate or to improve upon."

My three-year-old daughter, Madeline, recently demonstrated to me just how much wildlife information young children can assimilate. Madeline accompanied me during much of my fieldwork for my last book, the *Virginia Wildlife Viewing Guide*. In our travels, I often quizzed her on wildlife identification. Several months later, during Thanksgiving week, we returned to one of my favorite wildlife viewing locales, Chincoteague National Wildlife Refuge on Virginia's Eastern Shore, for a long weekend of hiking, biking, and wildlife watching. Chincoteague is a wildlife watcher's paradise. In autumn, hundreds of snow geese can be seen at one impoundment, aptly named Snow Goose Pool. During early fall, Chincoteague is one of the best places in the United States to view peregrine falcons.

Madeline and I attended a decoy festival held in the town of Chincoteague, as it is each year. World-class woodcarvers from up and down the East Coast show and sell their magnificent decoys and sculptures. My daughter walked up to one booth where a gentleman sat sculpting a decoy, making sure of the accuracy of his work.

"You know what this is?" he asked Madeline, simply looking for something to say to the child standing in front of his booth.

"Yes," she replied. "It's a Canada goose."

The eyebrows of the woodcarver rose slightly. He pointed to another decoy. "What's this one?"

"A redhead," quickly came the reply.

His curiosity was piqued. "What's this one?"

"A wood duck," Madeline said, "a boy wood duck." Then she turned and said to me, "This man doesn't know about ducks, Daddy."

THE NATIONAL WATCHABLE WILDLIFE PROGRAM

Wildlife managers across North America have noticed increasing numbers of wildlife enthusiasts. These managers have enhanced wildlife viewing opportunities in parks, refuges, forests, and wildlife management areas by constructing blinds and towers, building boardwalks through wetlands, and establishing wildlife viewing trails. They have also spread the word by producing wildlife viewing guides. These efforts have culminated in the establishment of the National

11

Watchable Wildlife Program, a historic partnership of state and federal conservation agencies and private conservation groups.

The National Watchable Wildlife Program encourages wildlife viewing, teaches people about wildlife, and increases public support for wildlife habitat acquisition and protection. *Sports Illustrated* magazine called the initiative "one of the most significant nationwide wildlife programs since the Endangered Species Act was signed." One goal of the program is a nationwide network of wildlife viewing sites, which will include natural areas known to offer excellent wildlife viewing and, in some cases, educational opportunities.

More than twenty states now participate in the national initiative. As you travel along the roads in these areas, look for highway signs featuring a pair of brown and white binoculars. These signs direct you to prime wildlife viewing areas that are part of the National Watchable Wildlife Program. Each viewing site you visit is just one of many in that state. Chances are, that state has published a wildlife viewing guide, with directions on how to get to each site and viewing information for anywhere from fifty to one hundred fifty other viewing areas. If you want to know if your state participates in the program, call your regional fish and wildlife agency. Or visit a local bookstore, and say you're interested in obtaining one of the state-by-state wildlife viewing guides published by Falcon Press.

THE IMPACT OF WILDLIFE VIEWING

As more and more people discover the benefits of wildlife viewing, wildlife managers across the nation have become concerned about the impact increased numbers of wildlife watchers have on the animals they wish to view.

People sometimes trample habitats and harass animals as they attempt to get a closer look or make animals "do" something. Even a few wildlife photographers get too close to bird nests or pursue animals for better shots, sometimes relentlessly; one photographer was seen throwing stones at perched birds so they could be photographed flying.

Viewers with good intentions can cause great harm. Reports have it that a few years ago in California, a group of birders made their way through a grassy marsh toward the "kick-ee-doo" call of the secretive black rail, a tiny black marsh bird with white spots on its back and a chestnut nape. Moments later the calls stopped . . . the bird had been trampled to death by the birders! At Redwoods State Park, an elk disturbed by people swam into the ocean and drowned. Bighorn sheep have lost footing and tumbled to their

> The goal of wildlife viewing is to observe animals without interrupting their normal activities.

deaths while distracted by individuals trying to get too close. Recent research has revealed other serious problems as well, such as nest abandonment and desertion of important feeding areas, resulting from increased human pressure.

These situations do not have to be. Wildlife and people can coexist if wildlife viewers follow the simple guidelines set forth in this book.

Watching Wildlife was written to enhance your wildlife viewing experiences. It presents tips and techniques for observing wildlife, choosing equipment, and finding species in the wild. You'll learn about the important links between a species and its habitat and how the daily and seasonal movements of wildlife relate to viewing success. But the most important parts of the book are the sections on appropriate wildlife viewing behavior. Most wildlife viewing takes place in wild areas, where there is no audience to approve (or disapprove) of conduct. Perhaps Aldo Leopold said it best when he

13

wrote, "Whatever his acts, they are dictated by his own conscience, rather than by a mob of onlookers. . . . Voluntary adherence to an ethical code elevates self-respect of the sportsman, but it should not be forgotten that voluntary disregard of the code degenerates and depraves him."

This book talks about this code that protects our wild creatures. And it also tells you how and where to find them. So pack up your binoculars, spotting scopes, identification guides, cameras, and this guide; gas up your car or boat; lace up your hiking boots. Then head out to enjoy one of North America's fastest growing outdoor activities—*watching wildlife*.

TAKE A CHILD WILDLIFE WATCHING

*M*ost environmental educators and psychologists agree that adult attitudes toward the natural world are greatly influenced by childhood events. And nothing seems to foster positive attitudes toward wildlife better than direct participation in wildlife-related activities, as the following examples show:

In a study on youth and their attitudes toward wildlife, researchers from the U.S. Fish and Wildlife Service found that children who actively watched birds, fished, or hunted knew more about wildlife and the natural world than children who did not participate in these activities.

Dr. Stephen Kellert of Yale University reported that children who only learned about wildlife in classrooms or zoos had the least real knowledge about animals and had a far less ecological perspective than other children. Kellert concluded that learning about animals in school needs to be supplemented by direct encounters with animals and natural habitats, whenever possible, to impart a deeper understanding of wildlife to children.

Studying a group of Florida eighth graders, Dr. David LaHart found an important link between positive attitudes toward wildlife and wildlife-oriented activities such as camping, fishing, birding, and hunting. Of all the variables he examined, LaHart ➤

found that children who participated in hiking, birding, and wildlife photography exhibited the most actual wildlife knowledge. He also discovered that class field trips produced far greater wildlife knowledge than did filmstrips, class lectures, reading, or watching television shows about wildlife.

"Reverence and respect are hard to teach," notes Cheryl Riley of the National Wildlife Federation. "They must follow from seeing, doing, and understanding, by becoming involved."

The future of North America's wildlife depends on our children's commitment to wildlife conservation. So take a child wildlife watching. Collect bugs and butterflies with your nephew. Explore the deep woods with your daughter. Introduce children to the mysteries and beauties of the natural environment. It's fun; it's also a learning experience. You will be helping a child develop positive feelings toward wildlife that will last a lifetime.

If a child is to keep alive his inborn sense of wonder . . . He needs the companionship of at least one adult who can share it, rediscovering with him the joy, excitement, and mystery of the world we live in.

RACHEL CARSON

2 | Safe
and Responsible
Viewing

Several years ago an article in the *National Parks and Conservation* magazine caught my attention:

> *During the second weekend in September, Denali National Park recorded the largest amount of traffic in the park's history. More than 1,000 vehicles passed through the Savage Creek Check Station of this remote Alaskan park.*
>
> *One of the main attractions of the drive through Denali is the number of animals—grizzlies, moose, Dall sheep, and caribou—that can be seen from the comfort of a vehicle. Park rangers noted, however, that the September traffic caused wildlife to retreat to quieter sections of the park. Also, vehicles killed a kit fox and a full-curl Dall sheep ram; and a line of camera-*

happy tourists and their cars prevented a grizzly from crossing the road.

What was anticipated to be an enjoyable and exciting weekend of wildlife viewing turned into something quite different—especially for the wildlife.

Unfortunately the situation at Denali that weekend was not an isolated event. Deborah Richie, Watchable Wildlife Coordinator for The Nature Conservancy/USDA Forest Service, recently wrote about problems caused by tourists, hikers, campers, and wildlife watchers at Glacier National Park in Montana. During the past decade, Richie noted, "Park rangers killed twenty-three black bears, seven grizzly bears, two mountain lions, a white-tailed deer, a mule deer, and a pine marten involved in conflicts with visitors. Twenty-one people suffered injuries from grizzly bears, and three [people] died."

Seeing humpback whales breach the warm waters of the Pacific, watching orcas slice through the glass surface of an Alaskan bay, counting hundreds of snow geese on their wintering grounds—these are the privileges of wildlife viewing. With these privileges, however, comes responsibility: the responsibility to observe wild animals without disrupting or interfering with their feeding, resting, or mating behaviors.

17

THE CHALLENGE OF WILDLIFE VIEWING

Your goal as a wildlife viewer is to observe animals without interrupting their normal activities. Meeting this challenge also provides the greatest satisfaction. When you watch without causing a reaction, you are seeing what's truly "wild" and not causing undue harm or stress to the animal in front of you.

In many ways, this notion of leaving animals alone conflicts with messages we receive from our culture. We have seen television hosts closely interact with and even touch wild animals. We have visited petting farms where domesticated animals eat from the outstretched hands of children. And we've safely stood and watched only a few feet away from large, dangerous animals in zoos. These activities in no way resemble appropriate interactions with wildlife in the field. Zoos and petting farms force animals into our world. Wildlife viewing, on the other hand, immerses us in the animals' world.

Wildlife biologists have documented many situations in which overzealous wildlife watchers caused serious problems for the animals they were interested in viewing. The reason for this problem is that some viewers think only of their single encounter with an animal, not in terms of cumulative impact. It's critical, however, to consider not only your encounter with an animal, but the impact of all those encounters that preceded it, and all that will follow.

Here are some reasons wildlife biologists are concerned with inappropriate human-wildlife interactions:

■ On Lake Huron, researchers found that human visits to tern colonies resulted in losses of eggs to predation by gulls.

■ Analysis of data collected from Cornell University's Laboratory of Ornithology revealed that predators often follow human trails to bird nests.

■ Disturbance by hikers and picnickers in the Santa Rosa Mountains in California caused desert bighorn sheep to abandon an important water hole.

■ Studies of brown pelicans and Heermann's gulls on the coast of

18

Baja California showed that disturbances by recreationists seriously disrupts seabird breeding.

■ In the Gulf of Maine, boats landing or passing too close to rocky islands have caused harbor seals to become restless; some adult seals have even abandoned their pups.

■ Human disturbance in the Gulf of Maine has frightened colonial nesting birds, resulting in nest abandonment, and leaving eggs and chicks susceptible to predation.

■ On the Madison River in Yellowstone National Park, photographers disturbed nesting trumpeter swans to such an extent that the birds left their nests.

■ Nesting shorebirds such as piping plovers and terns protect their eggs from the sun by sitting on them. When human activity forces a nesting shorebird to leave its nest for an undue length of time, the developing embryos can die from overheating. On a hot day, embryos can die in three minutes or less!

■ Human disturbance can cause birds of prey to abandon their nests, leaving young to die of starvation or exposure.

■ Human disturbance of Indiana bats and other bat species that hibernate in caves is a major cause of population declines.

■ Just touching coral causes damage to this fragile animal. Well-intentioned snorkelers and divers have unwittingly allowed hands, knees, fins, and tanks to contact coral, causing irreparable damage to reefs.

■ The eggs of the threatened piping plover are so well camouflaged that many unsuspecting wildlife viewers have stepped on and crushed them.

■ At Glacier National Park in Montana, ardent wildlife watchers have caused mountain goat kids to become separated from their mothers. This can happen several times a week. Unable to nurse as frequently as necessary, the goat kids lose the strength they need to escape danger. Other times, kids have run into oncoming traffic after being frightened by wildlife viewers.

No wildlife viewer wants to play a part in any of these incidents. Most inappropriate actions occur for two reasons. First, the thrill of the moment often pushes enthusiastic wildlife viewers to get closer and closer to animals. Second, some viewers just don't understand the long-term impacts of their actions. Perhaps the best advice comes from the California Department of Fish and Game, which suggests, "Always ask yourself, 'Will my presence or actions here harass some creature or displace it from its home? Is it okay for me to be here?' There's a fine line between viewing and victimizing wildlife." The Alaska Department of Fish and Game makes another important point. It notes, "Alarm cries and displays are an animal's request that you keep away."

Research indicates that wildlife's tolerance of people varies by species, season, reproductive and nutritional state, and by the degree to which the animals are accustomed to humans. Remember, energy that an animal uses to escape disturbances made by people is no longer available for other activities, such as escaping predators, attracting a mate, migrating, or raising young. Although the animal might easily compensate for a single, short disturbance, repeated disturbances add up to higher and higher energy costs. The animal may not be able to afford losing so much energy.

WILDLIFE WARNING SIGNS

Communication plays an important role in the lives of wild animals, just as it does in our world. To avoid placing wildlife in jeopardy, you need only watch and listen—if you do something inappropriate, the animal will usually let you know. Here are some of the signals used by wild animals to tell us when they feel threatened or disturbed:

Universal signals. Animals will:

■ Walk or run away (or fly, crawl, slither, hop, or swim away)

- Charge or threaten viewers
- Stop feeding
- Raise their heads and look at the disturbance
- Appear nervous
- Suddenly stand up from a resting position
- Change their direction of travel

Some signals used by mammals:

- Looking at you with their ears pointed in your direction
- White-tailed deer stomp their feet
- Woodchucks and marmots whistle
- Pronghorn antelope flare their white rump patches
- Beavers slap their tails on the water
- Grizzly bears may charge, and have killed people who come too close

Some signals used by birds:

- Exhibiting a "broken-wing" display
- Circling repeatedly
- Crying out overhead
- Diving at intruders
- Freezing
- Ducks pump their heads
- Young owls sway from side to side and "pop" their beaks
- Canada geese hiss and charge

JOHN JAMES AUDUBON, ARTIST AND WILDLIFE VIEWER

For a perfect conception of their beauty and elegance, you must observe them [trumpeter swans] when they are not aware of your proximity, as they glide over the waters of some secluded island pond. The neck, which at other times is held stiffly upright, moves in graceful curves, now bent forward, now inclined backwards over the body. The head, with an extended scooping movement, dips beneath the water, then with a sudden effort it throws a flood over its back and wings, while the sparkling globules roll off like so many large pearls. The bird then shakes its wings, beats the water, and, as if giddy with delight, shoots away, gliding over and beneath the surface of the stream with surprising agility and grace. Imagine a flock of fifty [trumpeter] swans thus sporting before you. I have more than once seen them, and you will feel, as I have felt, happier and freer of care than I can describe.

JOHN JAMES AUDUBON

THE GOLDEN RULES OF WATCHING WILDLIFE

Respect wildlife.
Respect wildlife habitat.
Respect other wildlife viewers and property.
Respect the WILD in wildlife

RESPECT WILDLIFE

The welfare of wildlife must always come first. To respect the wild animals and birds you view, follow these guidelines:

View wild animals from an appropriate distance. Always be aware of the distance between you and the animal you are watching—for the animal's protection and, in many cases, for your own. An appropriate viewing distance depends upon various factors, including the particular species, the temperament of the individual animal, and even the time of day and time of year of the encounter. A cow moose with young in spring is particularly dangerous. A nesting bird is especially susceptible to human disturbance.

What is an "appropriate" distance? Many national parks and refuges maintain viewing distance guidelines for selected species; check with a ranger or the visitor center before you take to the field. In many other places, however, you will have to judge the appropriate viewing distance on your own. In this situation, the primary rule is to view from a distance the animal feels comfortable with. Closely observe the animal for any of the warning signs described earlier. Has it stopped feeding? Is it acting skittish or nervous? If the answer is yes, you are too close.

Don't depend completely on warning signs, however. Some animals, such as bison, will charge without benefit of a warning. Be sure you are far enough away to avoid any sudden charges. (See page 27 for more on viewing large animals.)

The best way to bridge the distance between you and wild animals is to use binoculars, spotting scopes, and zoom lenses.

Stay clear of nests, dens, and rookeries; they are especially vulnerable to human disturbance. Many parent birds will abandon a nest with eggs if they are repeatedly flushed; there is a higher likelihood of predation if the parent is away from the nest. Flushed birds also give visual clues to predators about a nest's location; many predators follow human scents to nests.

Predators are not the only danger; some frightened birds refuse to feed their young. Nesting herons often regurgitate food when disturbed and numerous young herons have died of starvation as a result.

Use calls or whistles selectively. Calls, whistles, and recordings interrupt an animal's normal routine. Use calls selectively, and only with common species. Never use calls during times of mating or times of stress, such as winter.

Artificial calls are not allowed in national parks.

Never touch "orphaned" or sick animals, or wildlife that appears to be tame. Young wild animals that appear to be alone usually have parents waiting nearby.

Limit your stay. Most encounters with people stress an animal, even if no outward signs are visible. Like any good visitor, limit your stay and let the animal get back to its normal routine.

Avoid surprising wildlife. Never try to sneak up on an animal. A startled animal is stressed, and potentially dangerous. Sneaking up on an animal puts you in a predatory role, so you will be treated as a predator by that animal.

Don't litter. Litter is ugly and no one wants to look at it. But there's another reason not to litter: animals may eat the garbage left on the ground, whether it is edible or not. Since most human litter is from food and food wrappings, the garbage smells like something to eat. Animals will try to do so, but often become ill and die.

Animals also can become entangled in litter. Six-pack holder rings from soft drinks or beer are particularly disastrous. One of the most pathetic sights I ever witnessed was a Canada goose with its head stuck in one of these holders, thrashing about and choking.

Trash and food scraps on beaches where piping plovers nest attract predators that prey on plover eggs and chicks. Predation is a major reason for this beautiful bird's decline.

Burying garbage and food is a form of littering. Pack out what you pack in.

Leave pets at home. Your pets will startle, chase, and even kill wildlife. Do not bring them into the wild.

Not only do pets decrease your chances of seeing wildlife, you may also be placing your pet in jeopardy, since wild animals have been known to maim and kill pets while being harassed.

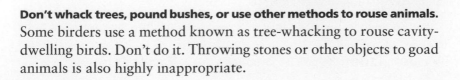

Don't whack trees, pound bushes, or use other methods to rouse animals. Some birders use a method known as tree-whacking to rouse cavity-dwelling birds. Don't do it. Throwing stones or other objects to goad animals is also highly inappropriate.

Never feed wild animals [see page 31].

RESPECT WILDLIFE HABITAT

When you watch wildlife outdoors, you enter an animal's home. Keep in mind the impacts you may be having on wildlife habitat, and minimize your effect by doing the following:

Stay on the trail. Using existing trails and pathways minimizes habitat trampling. Staying on trails also decreases your chances of getting lost. Don't take shortcuts across switchbacks when hiking in hilly or mountainous country; this damages vegetation and causes soil erosion.

Staying on trails also helps you to walk more quietly, increasing your likelihood of seeing wildlife.

Use restrooms. Human waste is a serious pollutant. It's important to think of it in terms of cumulative impact: urine along trails and roadsides can create salt concentrations that attract animals and habituate them to people. This is a problem in many national parks, including Glacier. Schedule and plan restroom visits, especially when in large groups.

Do not rearrange or disturb foliage around dens or nests. Don't rearrange foliage for a better view of a nest or den. By making a den or nest more visible to people, you also make it more visible to predators.

Leave the habitat better than you found it. Carry along a trash bag and pick up litter when you see it. I'll never forget watching herpetologist David Cook scale down several large boulders to pick up someone else's garbage while on a wildlife watching trip; he didn't think anyone else was watching as he quietly placed the litter in his pack. We can all learn from his actions.

RESPECT OTHER WILDLIFE VIEWERS AND PROPERTY

Wildlife viewing is a popular activity; don't be surprised if you encounter other people in the field. A little cooperation will go a long way. Keep the following tips in mind:

Respect the rights of others while in the field. If you approach too closely and scare an animal away, you ruin everyone's wildlife viewing experience. Large groups can schedule periods of silence so that animals are not frightened.

Don't monopolize the sightlines. If viewing in a crowd, take a look at the animal being observed, then let the next person have a turn.

Respect the rights of landowners. Always get permission before entering private property. Be courteous and leave gates and other property as you found them.

Spread the word about appropriate wildlife watching behavior. Teach others, especially children, about the importance of not disturbing wildlife while viewing.

Respect the WILD in Wildlife

Keep your distance from all animals, especially large ones such as bears, moose, mountain lions, alligators, and bison. Don't be lulled into a false sense of security by other people moving closer and closer to an animal, and don't think you are somehow protected because you are in a park or refuge.

Wild animals are just that—wild. These tips on respecting wild animals will help you enjoy your wildlife watching experience:

Do not approach large animals. In general, maintain a distance of at least one hundred yards from large mammals. Moose, bison, and bears can run at speeds of thirty-five miles per hour. The Center for Wildlife Information warns, "Moose will charge—running, kicking, and stomping—when they feel threatened. It only takes a small provocation (a person's approach, a dog's bark, or the scent of a coyote) to change a passive moose into a dangerous one."

Regarding bison, the Center notes, "Buffalo may look slow but are very fast. They also have short tempers. Buffalo will stomp, and use their horns and their massive body weight to gore or otherwise injure what they consider a threat."

Don't learn the hard way. Keep your distance.

Stay clear of a mother with young. No matter what, never approach a mother with young. Never allow yourself to get between a sow bear and her cubs; mother black bears warn their cubs of danger with a "woof," then turn to what they see as a threat. A cow moose also can become one of the most dangerous animals when protecting her young. During spring, be safe and assume a female moose, deer, or bear has young hidden nearby, and move away immediately.

Never surround an animal with a group of people. Large groups of people, led by the thrill of the moment, often surround an animal they are observing. Large mammals have been known to charge right through such crowds because they feel cornered, causing major injuries to wildlife watchers. Always give animals a way to escape.

Be aware of tides. While viewing in coastal areas, always be aware of tidal conditions. "Incoming tides can cut off your return route," notes the National Park Service. Never attempt to beat the tide.

Practice safety during hunting season. Fourteen million Americans and almost two million Canadians enjoy hunting each year. If you decide to view wildlife in areas where hunting is taking place, follow the same safety rules that hunters follow, such as wearing hunter orange. Since animals are much more wary during hunting season anyway, making wildlife observation more difficult, consider finding an alternative area where hunting is not allowed, such as a national park or urban refuge.

Know how to act around black bears, grizzly bears, and mountain lions. The chances of a negative encounter with a mountain lion, grizzly bear, or black bear, are exceedingly small. In fact, the chances of even **seeing** a mountain lion are low, even for the most experienced backcountry traveler. If you do encounter a mountain lion or bear, stay safe.

The Colorado Division of Wildlife notes that there are no definite rules about what to do if you meet a black bear or mountain lion, and that every situation is different, but it offers the following advice.

If you meet a mountain lion:

■ Do not approach it, especially one that is feeding or with kittens. Most mountain lions will try to avoid a confrontation.

■ Give it a way to escape.

■ Stay calm.

■ Talk calmly yet firmly to the lion.

■ Move slowly. Stop, then back away slowly, only if you can do so safely. Running may stimulate a lion's instinct to chase and attack.

■ Face the lion and stand upright, doing all you can to appear larger. Raise your arms and open your jacket if you're wearing one.

■ If you have small children with you, protect them by picking them up so they won't panic and run.

■ If the lion behaves aggressively, throw stones, branches, or whatever you can get your hands on without crouching or turning your back. Wave your arms slowly and speak firmly.

What you want to do is convince the lion you are not prey, and that you may in fact be a danger to the lion. Fight back if a lion attacks you.

If you meet a black bear:

■ Stay calm. If the bear hasn't seen you, calmly leave the area. As you move away, talk aloud to make the bear aware of your presence.

■ Back away slowly while facing the bear. Avoid direct eye contact, since bears may perceive this as a threat.

■ Give the bear plenty of room to escape. Wild bears rarely attack people unless they feel threatened or provoked.

■ If on a trail, step off the trail on the downhill side and slowly leave the area. Don't run or make any sudden movements. Running is likely to prompt the bear to give chase and you can't outrun a bear.

■ Speak softly. This may reassure the bear that no harm is meant to it.

■ Try not to show fear.

Bears use all their senses to try to identify what you are. Their eyesight is good and their sense of smell is excellent. If a bear stands upright or moves closer, it may be trying to detect smells in the air. This is not a sign of aggression. Once the bear identifies you, it may leave the area or try to intimidate you by charging to within a few feet before it withdraws. Fight back if a black bear attacks you.

The situation changes if you meet a grizzly bear. The Interagency Grizzly Bear Committee, the U.S. Fish and Wildlife Service, and the Wyoming Game and Fish Department teamed up to offer the following advice.

If you meet a grizzly in the backcountry:

■ First, try to back out of the situation. Keep calm, avoid direct eye contact, back up slowly, and speak in a monotone. Never turn your back on the bear and never kneel. Never run, and do not climb a tree unless you have time to climb at least ten feet before the bear reaches you. Remember, bears can run very fast. If you do have time to climb a tree, you may want to drop a nonfood item, such as a camera, to distract the bear while you climb.

■ If the bear charges, stand your ground. Bears often "mock charge" or run past you. The bear may charge several times before leaving the area. Shooting a bear when it is charging is not recommended. The bear almost always lives long enough to maul the shooter severely.

■ As a last resort, play dead. Curl into a ball, covering your neck and head with your hands and arms. If you have a backpack, leave it on; it will help protect your back. If the bear swats at you, roll with it. Stay in a tucked position and do not look at the bear or your surroundings until you are sure it is gone. Playing dead will not work in an encounter with a grizzly bear in camp.

WHY NOT FEED THE ANIMALS?

The sign reads PLEASE DO NOT FEED THE ANIMALS. But why not?

Feeding wild animals is fun, especially for children, isn't it? Wild animals like potato chips, don't they? Why shouldn't I feed those "hungry" animals? It's no big deal, is it?

Yes, it is. There are many good reasons for never feeding wild animals:

Animals that are fed by humans learn to associate people with food. Wild animals that become dependent on handouts often approach cars, making them more likely to be hit by vehicles. Hundreds of animals are struck by cars each year in parks and refuges as they approach for an easy meal.

When potentially dangerous animals associate people with food, disaster can strike. Consider the following from Florida's *Saint Petersburg Times*:

Some residents of the Port Charlotte subdivision where a four-year-old girl was killed by an alligator on Saturday had frequently fed marshmallows to gators in the area, a state wildlife official said Monday.

"We overheard one individual in the crowd that was there that night [when the girl died] *talking about how that gator*

31

looked like the one he had been feeding," said Lieutenant Jim Farrior of the Florida Game and Fresh Water Fish Commission.

Animals that are fed by humans lose their natural fear of people. Wild animals unafraid of people are more likely to be involved in harmful interactions, biting, kicking, or attacking wildlife viewers. When this happens, the offending animal loses—it is usually destroyed. In Yellowstone National Park, many people have been seriously injured and some have even been killed as a result of people feeding bears. One Yellowstone black bear was killed accidentally by a rubber bullet fired by a ranger to scare it away from a heavily used section of the park: the bear had been lured to the area with food by a wildlife photographer interested in "getting a good shot."

Animals that are fed by humans can destroy the environment. At Crater Lake National Park in Oregon, people feeding golden-mantled ground squirrels and birds have contributed to the erosion of the rim of this strikingly beautiful lake. Well-fed on potato chips, cheese curls, and raisins, the park's birds and squirrels have dramatically reduced their consumption, collection, and storage of pine seeds. Under natural conditions, these animals collect pine seeds and thus help distribute and plant the next generation of trees along the lake. The trees stabilize

the soil, preventing erosion. Now that more potato chips are eaten, fewer seeds are gathered, and there are fewer pine trees stabilizing the rim. The National Park Service at Crater Lake notes, "The [natural] chain has been broken."

Animals that are fed by humans cause property destruction. In Yosemite National Park in California, bears conditioned to human food cause almost $200,000 in property damage per year. Who knows?—your car, cabin, and camping or hiking equipment might be next.

Animals that are fed by humans may become unnaturally distributed in the environment. Studies conducted at Canyonlands and Arches national parks in Utah indicate that additional food at campgrounds has led to unnatural mammal distributions, disrupting the natural balance of the ecosystem.

Animals that are fed by humans are more likely to eat plastic wrappers and other litter. Eating litter can seriously harm an animal's digestive system, and in many cases leads to the animal's death.

Animals that are fed by humans can spread disease. Animals can carry diseases, such as bubonic plague or rabies, that can be transmitted to humans.

Animals that are fed by humans often are malnourished and forget how to find natural food for themselves. In some cases, wild animals that habitually eat human food lose their ability to digest natural food, and may become malnourished.

Wild animals fed by humans often become dependent on handouts. When the unnatural food source disappears, as it frequently does when park visitation diminishes in winter, such animals face starvation.

Animals that are fed by humans are more likely to become victims of poaching. Wild animals that become used to handouts are more likely to approach people, increasing their odds of becoming the victims of poachers.

It's illegal. In many states, feeding certain species is a criminal act punishable by fines and/or imprisonment. Feeding wildlife in national parks and refuges is illegal.

Feeding wildlife is a no-win situation. Please don't feed the animals!

MULE DEER AT GRAND CANYON ARE DYING TO BE FED

*I*n Grand Canyon National Park, park rangers have been forced to kill mule deer that become hooked on junk food left by hikers and campers. The deer develop extreme addictions to junk food and lose their ability to digest natural vegetation. Left in extremely poor health, the deer must be killed. According to David Haskell, chief of resource management at Grand Canyon National Park, junk food is "the crack cocaine of the deer world."

3 | Gear up:
Essentials and
Planning

Nothing will make you a better wildlife watcher than learning all you can about wildlife behavior and habitat; this knowledge is the very best wildlife viewing "gear" you can own. You'll then be ready to accentuate the positive by acquiring the right maps, clothes, and equipment.

Whether a wildlife viewing trip lasts a day or a week, careful planning and the right gear pays off in terms of comfort, time saved, and viewing success. Since many viewing locales are remote and have no facilities, wildlife watchers should review information about an area before a visit, checking for warnings about roads, seasonal closures, dangerous wildlife, and available facilities. Make reservations

for wildlife tours or request access to restricted areas well in advance. Many people enjoy wildlife viewing, and wildlife tours and sites are in great demand.

MAPS

Always bring along good maps. Most state tourism departments offer free state maps, and you may purchase a DeLorme Atlas & Gazetteer for your state. These atlases include topographic maps that include most back roads. DeLorme maps are sold in many stores and catalogs; you may also buy one by calling (800) 227-1656 and asking for individual atlas sales. Obtain site maps from the park or refuge managers.

Ask questions about the area you plan to visit. Site managers can tell you most of what you need to know. Most travel destinations have convention and visitors bureaus that offer free information on accommodations, restaurants, campgrounds, and more. Many of these visitors bureaus have teamed up with state fish and wildlife agencies and other conservation groups to develop materials about local wildlife viewing.

THE FALCON PRESS WATCHABLE WILDLIFE® SERIES

Falcon Press of Helena, Montana, has teamed up with Defenders of Wildlife, state and federal resource agencies, and other conservation organizations to produce a series of state-specific wildlife viewing guides. Currently available for twenty-one states, these guides feature the best wildlife viewing sites in each state, with specific information on the types of wildlife most likely to be observed and the times of year various species may be seen. You'll also find directions to each site and important information on facilities. Color photos in each guide highlight popular wildlife species. Plus, a portion of the proceeds goes to wildlife conservation efforts.

To order, or for more information, contact Falcon Press Publishing Company, P.O. Box 1718, Helena, MT 59624; phone (800) 582-2665.

FIELD GUIDES

Field guides help you positively identify many of the animals you will see. Look for field guides on birds, mammals, reptiles, amphibians, fish, trees, plants, and wildflowers. The Peterson, Audubon, and Golden field guide series are the most popular and most informative guidebooks. I am often asked which series is the best. My answer is that I could not get by without any of them.

The Peterson field guide series is excellent for immediate identification—arrows and italics provide at-a-glance identification of each species' distinctive field marks. The Audubon series features color photographs and organizes species by habitat type. Golden guides have range maps on the same page as the species drawings, helping readers find what plants and animals inhabit their region.

Other reference books can be as valuable. The National Geographic Society *Field Guide to the Birds*, for instance, is an excellent guide with exquisite illustrations.

CHECKLISTS

Many parks and refuges produce checklists of animals found within their boundaries. Many state fish and wildlife agencies also produce checklists of wildlife within their state or region. Checklists contain information on what species occur, when they occur, how common they are during each season, and whether they nest or live on the site.

To get one of these invaluable checklists, call or write the location you will be visiting and ask to have one mailed to you. Or ask for a checklist at the visitor center/ranger station when you arrive, or get one from your state fish and wildlife agency. Checklists usually are available for birds, mammals, amphibians and reptiles, and fish.

LIFE LISTS

Many wildlife watchers, especially birders, keep a list of wildlife species they have seen. Often referred to as "life lists," these may be simple listings of species observed or more elaborate notated lists, including such information as season, date, time, location, habitat type, weather conditions, and behavior of the animal. Taking field notes requires careful observation and helps you learn about different species.

OTHER SOURCES OF WILDLIFE VIEWING INFORMATION

Wildlife viewing information has proliferated during the past five years. Much of this information is free. Contact your state fish and wildlife agency, or any of the large land management agencies listed below, for more information on "Watchable Wildlife."

National Parks

Yellowstone, Grand Canyon, Yosemite, Shenandoah . . . our national parks are some of the most beautiful places in North America, with 83 million acres of wildlife viewing opportunities. National parks are administered by the National Park Service of the U.S. Department of the Interior. Although some national parks are crowded in certain places, a one- or two-mile hike off the beaten path will often lead to less crowded, even remote areas. National parks tend to be heavily used at certain times of the year and virtually empty at others. Plan your trip accordingly and enjoy our national park system, the envy of the world. For more information about our national parks, contact the National Park Service, Interior Building, P.O. Box 37127, Washington, DC 20013-7127; phone (202) 208-6843.

Watching Wildlife

The National Wildlife Refuge System

The U.S. Fish and Wildlife Service is the principal agency through which the federal government carries out its responsibilities to conserve, protect, and enhance the nation's fish and wildlife and manage their habitats for the continuing benefit of people. The National Wildlife Refuge System is managed by the U.S. Fish and Wildlife Service to meet this goal. As a network of more than 90 million acres of land and water in the United States, it contains almost five hundred national wildlife refuges that provide critical wildlife habitat from Alaska to the Florida Keys, and from the Caribbean to the central Pacific.

Although almost every type of habitat is represented in the NWR system, most refuges are located along four major waterfowl migration flyways, providing important feeding and resting areas during spring and fall migrations. Besides their crucial role for migratory birds, the refuges are managed for protection of endangered plants and animals, preservation of diversity, and education—they serve as places for people to better understand and enjoy wildlife. For details about these protected lands, contact the U.S. Fish and Wildlife Service, 4401 North Fairfax Drive, Webb Building, MS 130, Arlington, VA 22203; phone (703) 358-1700.

Bureau of Land Management

The Bureau of Land Management manages almost half of all federally owned lands. The BLM's National Watchable Wildlife Program was designed to increase opportunities to photograph, study, or view more than three thousand wildlife species on 270 million acres of BLM-administered land. Current goals of the Watchable Wildlife Program are to promote enhanced opportunities to view and enjoy wildlife; promote learning about wildlife and its needs; and strengthen public support for wildlife conservation and management. For more information, contact the Bureau of Land Management, 1849 C Street NW, Washington, DC 20240; phone (202) 343-5717.

National Forests

The USDA Forest Service administers our national forests and

40

national grasslands. This agency is responsible for the management of resources on 191 million acres of land—an area about the size of Utah, Colorado, and Wyoming combined. National forests are habitat to more than ten thousand plant and three thousand wildlife and fish species.

The Forest Service's "NatureWatch" program enhances wildlife watching opportunities for people, helping them experience wildlife, fish, and plant resources. It also encourages the public to learn about and support conservation efforts. For details, contact the USDA Forest Service, P.O. Box 96090, Washington, DC 20090-6090; phone (202) 205-0957.

National Marine Sanctuaries

From the Hawaiian Islands Humpback Whale National Marine Sanctuary to the Florida Keys National Marine Sanctuary, the marine sanctuary system offers wildlife watchers numerous viewing opportunities in a marine environment. Its twelve sanctuaries are designed to promote comprehensive management of ecological, historical, recreational, and aesthetic resources.

The National Marine Sanctuaries are administered by the Sanctuaries and Reserves Division of the National Oceanic and Atmospheric Administration, U.S. Department of Commerce. The sanctuaries produce several excellent wildlife watching brochures; be sure to pick up the brochure on whale watching at the Hawaiian Islands Humpback Whale National Marine Sanctuary, (808) 541-3184, and the coral identification guide you can take underwater, produced in cooperation with The Nature Conservancy and the Florida Advisory Council on Environmental Education. Contact the National Oceanic and Atmospheric Administration, National Ocean Service, Sanctuaries and Reserves Division, 1305 East-West Highway, 12th Floor, Silver Spring, MD 20910; phone (301) 713-3074.

National Estuarine Research Reserve System

Estuaries are places where rivers meet the sea. The National Estuarine Reserve System is dedicated to fostering a system of estuary reserves that represents the wide range of coastal and estuarine habitats found in the United States. Currently the system provides 425,000

41

acres in seventeen states, all dedicated to protecting, managing, and providing excellent wildlife viewing opportunities. The system works with federal and state authorities to establish, manage, and maintain reserves, and to provide for their long-term stewardship. Contact: Sanctuaries and Reserves Division, Office of Ocean and Coastal Resource Management, National Oceanic and Atmospheric Administration, Washington, DC 20235; phone (202) 482-3384.

State Lands

Each state maintains a system of parks, forests, and wildlife management areas. Most state fish and wildlife agencies have developed areas for wildlife viewing and offer assistance for viewers who need more information. For example, the Colorado Division of Wildlife's Watchable Wildlife Program produces an enormous amount of information on how, when, and where to view wildlife; the Florida Game and Fresh Water Fish Commission's Nongame Wildlife Program publishes checklists of birds, mammals, reptiles, and amphibians, as well as a newsletter featuring wildlife viewing activities. Contact the fish and wildlife agency in your state or one you are planning on visiting. Generally, wildlife viewing material is available through the state government's nongame or watchable wildlife program.

SCENTS AND SUNGLASSES

When you view wildlife in warmer months, you often enter the domain of mosquitos, flies, ticks, chiggers, and other less-appealing creatures. Pack insect repellent. You'll need it.

Many animals have an excellent sense of smell, so wear unscented lotions when you can and limit the use of perfume and cologne. You may wish to mask your natural odors as well. Outdoor specialty shops sell scent blockers that inhibit human scent.

Wear sunglasses to protect your eyes from UV rays. Polarized sunglasses facilitate wildlife viewing in and around water, so can help you view fish and aquatic or marine mammals. Sunglasses also help you spot birds overhead. However, don't wear sunglasses that glint or shine when the sun hits them—they will alert animals to your presence.

PACKS AND BAGS

For longer trips, pack along a canteen of water and snacks. Daypacks are good for carrying these items. And don't forget to pack trash bags to carry out garbage—your own and that of others you may find on the trail.

CLOTHING

Poor clothing choices will leave you uncomfortable; you'll end up either cold, wet, or hot. Poorly chosen clothing may also frighten away animals. The following information will help you pack wisely.

It is always better to have too much clothing with you than not enough. You can get hypothermia in fifty-degree weather if it's windy and rainy and you are not dressed properly. Dressing well means being conscious of how quickly weather can change; I've started watching wildlife on a morning when it was 60 degrees Fahrenheit and returned in 30-degree weather!

Boots

A good pair of sturdy shoes or boots is essential if you watch wildlife in more rugged country. Never hike in new boots. To break them in before you hit the trail, walk a mile or two every other night around your neighborhood.

The type of boot you should purchase depends on where you will be going and what you will be doing. Generally the more difficult the terrain, the stiffer the sole of the boot should be. The stiffer the sole, the heavier the boot. Light boots are nice because they have less break-in time and tend to cost less; heavier boots provide more support. If you don't need the support of a heavy boot, choose something lighter. Lighter boots have less environmental impact, especially off trail.

All boots should fit snugly, offer good traction, and provide ankle support. Never buy ill-fitting boots. Base your decision on the advice of a knowledgeable person, such as one of the staff at an outdoor specialty shop, in conjunction with your own gut feeling. When you slip on a pair of boots that fit the way they should, you'll know it.

Socks

Layer socks to wick away moisture, provide cushioning, and hold in warmth. Some synthetic materials have been used to make socks of medium weight that do all three of these things.

Hats

You'll need a hat and sunscreen for wildlife viewing near the shore or in more open areas. A hat with a brim that hides your eyes is a good choice, since a pair of staring eyes often signals danger to a wild animal.

The best fabrics for warm weather hats are cotton and cotton/synthetic blends, because they are cooler. For cold weather, purchase something made from a synthetic fabric that breathes and is waterproof. Do not wear a winter hat made of cotton. Cotton is not water repellent; if it gets wet, it doesn't dry easily. Wool continues to breathe and keeps your head warm, but is not as comfortable as some synthetics. Whatever type of cold-weather hat you find, be sure to wear it. Much of your body heat can escape through the top of your head.

Colors and Camouflage

When selecting clothing to wear outdoors, choose colors that match your surroundings. Earth tones and drab colors—browns, greens, dark grays—work best in most environments; white parkas are excellent in snow. The key is to consider what you look like from an animal's point of view. In the woods, a white shirt sticks out like a sore thumb. Also consider the sounds your clothing makes: hard-surfaced synthetic fabrics tend to be noisy in the cold. Quieter clothing will not disturb wildlife.

You may wish to wear camouflage clothing in an environment where there are lots of broken shadows. Camouflage garb and fabric can be found in army surplus stores and outdoor specialty shops. Consider wearing camouflage gloves and hanging camo mesh from your hat to keep animals from seeing your eyes.

But remember that camouflage isn't meant to be used every day. Bob Hernbrode of the Colorado Division of Wildlife points out that it is a specialized fabric. He says, "Washing 'camo' with most household detergents can create clothing that, to the eyes of many wild animals, almost 'glows' in low-light situations. This is because the color brighteners in detergents enhance the ultraviolet (UV) part of the light and color spectrum, which many animals see better than we do." Hernbrode suggests using old-fashioned natural soaps, or soaps that mute the UV colors. These soaps can be purchased in outdoor supply houses or through catalogs.

Dressing in Layers

Dress in layers when you head outdoors for any length of time.

The first layer—the layer closest to your skin—should "wick" moisture away from the skin and keep you dry. This "wicking" layer can be long johns or light clothing made of a thin fabric, such as silk, Capilene polyester, hollow-core polyester, hydrophilic nylon, etc. For wicking away perspiration, Capilene is excellent.

Your second layer of clothing should act as insulation. Appropriate fabrics include some of the new synthetics, down, and wool. Wool is the traditional insulator, but it is not quite as good as newer fabrics when wet because it's heavy.

Your third layer should be windproof and waterproof. Gore-Tex is the most popular, waterproof, and breathable outdoor fabric, so many wildlife watchers use it. Other fabrics are equally waterproof but not so breathable, or vice-versa. For your windproof/waterproof layer, purchase a fabric that suits your primary activity best: buy something more waterproof for wet activities, more breathable for aerobic activities.

Don't forget to protect your extremities. Layer your gloves, too, or wear the type that wick, insulate, and repel wind and rain. And remember: dressing properly for warm weather is just as important as dressing for cold. In hot weather, consider the danger of sunstroke and overheating.

OPTICS

Binoculars and Spotting Scopes

A good pair of binoculars and a high-powered spotting scope are the two most important pieces of equipment a wildlife watcher can have. Binoculars and spotting scopes bridge the distance between you and a wild animal. You'll enjoy a better view while remaining a safe distance from wildlife, leaving animals undisturbed and keeping yourself safe.

Binoculars come in several sizes and degrees of magnification, such as 7 x 35, 8 x 40, and 10 x 50. The first number refers to how large the animal will be magnified compared to the naked eye. A "7x" figure, for example, means the animal is magnified seven times larger than it would be if you viewed it without binoculars. More magnification is not always better. Larger magnifications can amplify hand movements, making wildlife harder to see; a bird in a tree will be harder to find with a 10x magnification than with a 7x, because your small movements, even your breathing, will cause the image to move. The second number refers to the diameter of the large end of the lens (the end facing the animal). The greater that number, the greater the amount of light entering the lens—which means better viewing in dim light. A 7 x 50 pair of binoculars will produce an image approximately 1.5 times brighter than a 7 x 35 pair, though the 7 x 50 model will also be heavier. At one hundred feet, a 7 x 35 pair of binoculars will allow you to see an animal as if it were just fourteen feet away.

On some binoculars, you may notice a third number following the first two, expressed in degrees. This is the field of view that the binoculars cover (spotting scopes have a similar reading). The larger the field of view, the larger the area seen through the eyepiece.

There's no perfect pair of binoculars. When purchasing binoculars, consider in what conditions and circumstances they will be used, and choose accordingly. For example, pocket-size binoculars (such as size 8 x 21) are small and easy to carry. However, they do not work well in low light—but most animals are active in low light, and this is when the best wildlife viewing occurs. The most common size of binoculars chosen by wildlife watchers is 7 x 35; it strikes a reasonable balance between compact size and amount of light entering the lens.

Binoculars are relatively easy to use. First, locate the animal using your naked eye. Then bring the binoculars up to your eyes. If at first you don't succeed at finding your object in the lens, locate a larger object or landmark close to the animal with your naked eye. Make a mental note of where the animal is in relation to the large object. Bring the binoculars to your eyes again, find the larger object, then bring the animal into your field of vision.

Spotting scopes, which can be set on tripods, are used for viewing more stationary wildlife at long distances, such as animals tending a nest. Spotting scopes are monocular (having one lens) and feature much higher magnification than binoculars; you can see farther with them.

There are two types of
spotting scopes. Refractor
scopes are wide-angle, low-
magnification scopes for
viewing closer subjects. Catadioptric
scopes have a narrower field of view and
greater magnification. Catadioptric
scopes generally have lower-quality
resolution, so they are not as good
as refractor scopes for general use.

One of the best wildlife watching
memories I have is of watching nesting
bald eagles at Saint Marks National Wildlife
Refuge in Florida with a spotting scope. The scope was so powerful
I could see the eagle viewing me.

Night Vision Viewers

Originally designed for military and law enforcement use, night
vision viewers are used by wildlife viewers to open up a nocturnal
world and find previously unseen wildlife. Night vision viewers
monumentally enhance observation of such animals as bats, owls,
foxes, raccoons, and bears. Night goggles can provide some of the
greatest wildlife watching thrills.

Night vision viewers come in binocular and monocular forms,
and range in price from $400 for lower-quality Russian military
surplus products to more than $2,000 for higher-quality viewers. The
more expensive models reflect the latest optics
and electronics; some attachments have
zoom capabilities.

Be sure the viewer you select is water-
resistant, floats, and has the ability to resist
humidity and moisture, which can cause
internal fogging. Rupert Cutler, executive
director at Virginia's Explore Park in
Roanoke, has had staff lead nighttime wildlife

walks using night vision goggles for several years. Cutler points out that the same rules apply for nighttime watching as daytime watching: stay quiet and station yourself at a place frequented by wildlife.

Purchasing a night vision viewer is expensive; before you do so, study your options. Write away for information from various companies. One of the leaders in night vision viewers is ITT Night Vision, 7635 Plantation Road, Roanoke, VA 24019; phone (800) 448-8678.

Taking It to the Limit

The Iroquois National Wildlife Refuge in Alabama, New York, has taken wildlife watching with optics to new heights. Refuge officials have mounted two cameras in a bald eagle nesting tree; the cameras transmit live television pictures from the nest to a monitor in refuge headquarters. Eagles can be viewed during regular business hours. The birds lay their eggs in March; eaglets fledge in mid-July. For more information about this unique program, contact Iroquois National Wildlife Refuge, P.O. Box 517, 1101 Casey Road, Alabama, NY 14003; phone (716) 948-5445.

4 | Taking
to the
Field

No matter the time of day or time of year, North America always has wildlife to be observed, enjoyed, studied, and photographed. Fresh viewing opportunities arrive each day and each season, in every habitat and in every region. Some species, such as songbirds, ducks, hawks, and butterflies, are most active and best seen during the day. Others, such as owls, raccoons, bats, flying squirrels, and secretive bobcats, are most active at night.

Each hour brings diversity, and each season brings variety. Migrant songbirds arrive in spring from points south to nest and rear their young. Animals hidden all winter emerge from hibernation. In summer, when many of us take our vacations, deer feed in fields and teach their young to do the same. Fall means migration for many species;

for wildlife viewers, migration means unparalleled viewing opportunities. Wildlife viewing does not end with the arrival of winter. In fact, with the leaves off the trees, and wildlife in wintering grounds, winter can often be the best viewing season of all.

4 STEPS FOR SUCCESSFUL WILDLIFE VIEWING

I once entered Saint Marks National Wildlife Refuge in north Florida with hopes of seeing one of the many eagles that nest in the area. As I laced up my hiking boots at the Mounds Interpretive Trail, a very noisy group of people approached me. One young fellow was banging something and another young lady was talking at the top of her lungs. "Don't waste your time," one individual said, "There aren't any eagles back there."

Somewhat discouraged, I set out down the trail. Upon reaching one of my favorite spots, I sat to enjoy the wonderful view along the marsh, breathing in the salt air. Not five minutes later two bald eagles appeared in the distance and alighted, in plain view, on a snag about two hundred yards away. I set up my spotting scope and enjoyed one of the best eagle-watching days of my life—with the exception of slamming car doors, shouting, and shrieking in the distance as the group I had met in the parking lot made their grand exit.

Successful wildlife viewing doesn't just happen. You will greatly increase your chances of seeing wildlife by following some simple guidelines. Here are four basic steps for successful wildlife viewing:

1. *Look in the right place.*
2. *Look at the right time.*
3. *Develop wildlife viewing skills and techniques.*
4. *Understand the species and its habits.*

STEP ONE: LOOK IN THE RIGHT PLACE

If you want to see certain animals, you need to find out where—exactly—they live.

Each animal species is found only in a certain area, known as its range. White-tailed deer, for example, have a large range—you'll find them throughout most of the United States and southern Canada. Mule deer, on the other hand, live only in the western United States and southwest Canadian provinces—a smaller range. Black-tailed deer (a subspecies of mule deer) have a smaller range yet; they are found only in a narrow strip of woodlands and temperate coniferous forest along the Pacific Coast, from central California to Alaska.

An animal lives in a specific habitat within its range. A habitat is a place that provides the right combination of food, water, and cover a species needs for nesting, hiding, feeding, and sleeping. Habitat needs can vary greatly from one species to the next, even when the animals seem similar. Consider the red-tailed hawk and the red-shouldered hawk. To judge from their names, you might think these two birds are nearly identical. However, red-shouldered hawks prefer to live in swampy woods, where they feed mostly on snakes and frogs. Red-tailed hawks favor drier, open areas, such as fields and pasturelands, and feed mostly on small rodents. They prefer different habitats.

LIFE ON THE EDGE

Many animal species live on the edge.

An edge is any place where two different habitats meet, such as where a field meets a forest, or a pond meets cattails. Think of edges as transition zones where animals can feel safe. Deer and wild turkeys, for example, often feed in a field, but stay close to the forest where they can take cover if danger should appear.

Scan edge areas for wildlife. Look for standing dead trees: you'll have a good chance of seeing a hawk perched there, waiting for a rabbit or a mouse to enter the field.

Some species are extremely selective about habitat, while others can live in many places. For example, within their range (which includes most of North America), great horned owls can be found in a large number of different habitats, including forests, deserts, open country, and swamps. Great gray owls are much more selective within their northern range, living only in boreal coniferous forests and muskeg.

Most good field guides identify the preferred habitat of the animals you want to see. You can consult a field guide, then set out to locate that habitat on your next viewing trip. Recognizing the link between a species and its habitat is a fundamental lesson in successful wildlife viewing. It is also a lesson in wildlife conservation. Without its proper habitat, a wildlife species cannot exist. Habitat destruction and alteration are two of the greatest threats to North America's wildlife.

Here are examples of different habitats:

- Open ocean
- Seashore
- Salt marsh

■ Freshwater marsh
■ Lakes, ponds, rivers
■ Grassland
■ Deciduous forest
■ Coniferous forest

Here are some habitats with a few of the species you might see there:

■ Old growth forest, Oregon
Spotted owl, pine marten, northern goshawk, northern flying squirrel.

■ Sonoran Desert, Arizona
Desert bighorn sheep, javelina, large-eared kit fox, kangaroo rat, Gila woodpecker, elf owl, Gila monster, desert tortoise, zebra-tailed lizard.

■ Seashore, Assateague Island, Maryland–Virginia (summer)
Brown pelican, sanderling, semipalmated sandpiper, black skimmer, several species of gull (laughing, ring-billed, herring, and greater black-backed).

The link between habitats and wildlife can be illustrated with a hypothetical summer hike through a conifer forest in central New York. The hike meanders through various plant communities, and each community offers different wildlife viewing opportunities. The trail begins in a grassy area, then winds through low shrubs, and eventually goes through high shrubs. The high shrubs give way to a shrub-tree community, then the trail enters an opening. The trail then moves into an area of low trees. As the trail moves deeper into the forest, the trees get taller. The trail ends in a mature forest.

While we are lacing up our hiking boots in the early morning in the grassy area, a high pitched "kip-kip-kip" catches our attention. It is the song of the diminutive grasshopper sparrow. Looking back down at our boots, we are distracted by motion; we see a meadow jumping mouse scurrying for cover. Hiking toward the forest, we enter the shrub area where we observe a purple finch and listen to a song sparrow. Hiking away from the shrubby area and into the opening, we spot a white-tailed deer browsing. We cross into the low tree community and spot a Nashville warbler. Finally, in the mature forest, while we take a break on a fallen log, a veery—a tawny-colored thrush—flies by.

Each of these animals prefers a different kind of habitat. We would not likely have seen a veery in the grassy area where the hike began. And since the grasshopper sparrow likes open grassy and weedy meadows, it would probably not have been in the mature forest at trail's end. Some species might live in several of the natural communities along the trail. We might have seen an Eastern cottontail rabbit in the grassy areas, the shrub community, and in the forest opening, but it wouldn't be found in mature forest. We would not have observed red squirrels at the beginning of the hike, but might have watched them leap from tree to tree at the walk's end.

Elevation also plays an important role in wildlife viewing. Habitat and climate change with increasing elevation, affecting the wildlife community. The mammal population changes within several elevation

THERE'S LIFE IN THAT DEAD TREE

One of the best places to search for wildlife is in and around a snag.

A snag is a standing dead tree. Think of snags as animal condominiums. Hawks and eagles use snags because their few branches and no leaves provide prime vantage points for hunting prey. Cavity-nesting birds such as woodpeckers excavate holes in the decaying wood. Flying squirrels, nuthatches, bluebirds, bats, owls, and American kestrels use cavities abandoned by other animals, or make nests in natural holes that result from lost branches or lightning strikes. Squirrels use snags as a place to store food; insect-eating birds search for prey there.

There is life, and lots of it, in that dead tree.

57

zones and, with it, so do mammal viewing opportunities at Yosemite National Park in California. Here's an overview of where in Yosemite some mammals live:

■ Foothills: 500 to 3,000 feet
Western harvest mouse, dusky-footed wood rat, spotted skunk, mule deer, bobcat.

■ Lower montane: 3,000 to 6,000 feet
Deer mouse, California ground squirrel, western gray squirrel, California mole, valley pocket gopher, mink, ringtail, coyote, bobcat, mule deer, mountain lion, black bear.

■ Upper montane: 6,000 to 8,000 feet
Lodgepole chipmunk, bush-tailed wood rat, Douglas squirrel, northern flying squirrel, golden-mantled ground squirrel, yellow-bellied marmot, porcupine, long-tailed weasel, river otter, coyote, mule deer, black bear.

■ Subalpine: 8,000 to 11,000 feet
Water shrew, heather vole, belding ground squirrel, pika, mountain pocket gopher, mule deer (summer), bighorn sheep.

■ Alpine: 11,000 feet and above
Alpine chipmunk, alpine gopher, pika.

STEP TWO: LOOK AT THE RIGHT TIME

Timing is everything. Animal activity depends on the time of day and the time of year.

Some animals, such as songbirds, hawks, and red and gray squirrels, are active during the day (diurnal). Other species, such as owls, bats, raccoons, bobcats, flying squirrels, and opossums are active at night (nocturnal). In general, early morning and evening are the best times to view most birds and large mammals, since they are most active at these times. At midday, watch for hawks "kettling," circling and soaring on columns of rising warm air. Most amphibians and reptiles are active at night for three reasons. First, their prey—insects—are more active and plentiful then. Second, harsh sun rays can dry out reptiles' porous skin, such as that of salamanders. And third, darkness affords greater protection from predators.

Some wildlife species are present in particular areas only during certain times of the year. If you want to see the 7,500 elk at the National Elk Refuge in Jackson, Wyoming, go there in winter. If you visit in summer, those same elk will be in the high country, miles away.

Want to see bald eagles? Lots of bald eagles? Timing is everything. One of the largest concentrations of bald eagles in the lower forty-eight states occurs in winter at the Klamath Basin along the Oregon–California border. Most of the eagles there come from Canada for the winter, arriving in November and departing by April. More than five hundred eagles are present during January and February. For more information about this fine eagle site, contact Klamath Basin National Wildlife Refuge, Route 1, Box 74, Tule Lake, CA 96134;

1 Des Lacs NWR
   Upper Souris NWR
   J. Clark Salyer NWR

2 Devils Lake

3 Sand Lake NWR

4 DeSoto NWR

5 Squaw Creek NWR

North Dakota

South Dakota

Iowa

Missouri

phone (916) 667-2231. Or contact the Oregon Department of Fish and Wildlife, 1400 Miller Island Road, West Klamath Falls, OR 97603; phone (503) 883-5732.

Timing really matters if you want to witness spectacular wildlife displays during spring and fall migrations. Here's an example of how the timing of migration relates to viewing snow geese in the central United States (see map, opposite page): at Squaw Creek National Wildlife Refuge in northwestern Missouri, gatherings of up to 300,000 snow geese have been observed during their fall

"There is a direct correlation between seeing wildlife and spending enough time in the field."

-Mark Hilliard
Watchable Wildlife Coordinator
Bureau of Land Management

migration in October and November. Where did all of these geese come from? Most of the snow geese seen at Squaw Creek spend summers breeding and raising young along the west coast of the Hudson Bay. Between August and October, as the arctic summer comes to a close, the geese begin migrating south in flocks of 100 to 1,000. They fly between forty and fifty miles per hour at altitudes of around 3,000 feet (although they have been recorded as high as 20,000 feet). Some of these birds fly nonstop to wintering grounds on the Gulf Coast or Mexico, but other flocks stop along the way.

Some of the first stops are the Des Lacs, Upper Souris, and J. Clark Salyer national wildlife refuges in northwest North Dakota. When inclement weather drives the geese from these areas, they continue south to Devils Lake Wetland Management District in east-central North Dakota, then go still farther south to Sand Lake, South Dakota. When cold drives the geese from Sand Lake, they move on to DeSoto National Wildlife Refuge in Iowa, then fly to Squaw Creek. As winter tightens its grip and the marshes at Squaw Creek freeze, the snow geese move again, this time to their wintering grounds along the Gulf Coast of Texas and Louisiana.

Here today, gone next week, or perhaps the week after.

For more information on the snow geese migration, contact Squaw Creek National Wildlife Refuge, P.O. Box 101, Mound City, MO 64470; phone (816) 442-3187.

Other Timing Issues to Consider

Hibernation

Some animals appear only at certain times of the year, but not because they migrate. These animals are sometimes out of sight because they hibernate, or become inactive during the winter season. The Columbian ground squirrels of Glacier National Park, for instance, are active and visible for only about five months of the year. Emerging from hibernation in April, they begin immediate preparations for the next winter, feeding on grasses, seeds, and other vegetation. They disappear by August or September and will hibernate for the next seven to eight months.

Tides

Tides affect wildlife viewing success. Most shorebirds and whales are best observed at high tides, while intertidal life can be explored during low tides.

Weather

Changes in weather can present wildlife viewing opportunities. After rain, many predators emerge to feed on displaced insects and rodents. Wetter, cooler weather associated with low-pressure systems can increase your chance of seeing animals. Many animals are active just after a storm, and wildlife seems less sensitive to noise and smell at that time.

The best time to view Florida manatees is in winter right after a cold front, when the manatees gather around the warm-water discharges of power plants and congregate at warm springs, such as those found in Kings Bay–Crystal River National Wildlife Refuge and Homosassa Springs State Wildlife Park.

Cold fronts often "push" migrating birds south in the fall. On September 14, 1978, more than 21,000 broad-winged hawks were spotted in one day over Hawk Mountain, Pennsylvania, as a massive cold front came down from Canada. The best viewing of bald eagles on the Upper Mississippi River National Wildlife and Fish Refuge in Winona, Minnesota, "occurs after periods of bitter weather, when

TAKING TO THE FIELD

ORNITHOLOGY 101

Ornithology—the study of birds—is one of the more difficult courses wildlife management students must pass to earn a degree. Students must identify hundreds of birds, learn dozens of bird songs, and memorize numerous scientific names. Such stress gives rise to a good number of amusing stories about ornithology courses.

One of the best stories I know involved a group of budding wildlife managers eager to take a midsemester exam focusing on bird identification. The well-prepared students walked into the classroom only to find all the mounted bird specimens covered with towels. Only the birds' feet were visible.

"What is this?" asked one startled student.

"What's going on here?" asked another.

Smiling, the professor explained that to be a truly outstanding ornithologist, one had to be able to identify birds using only the shapes of their feet. A silence fell upon the students, until one frustrated individual stood up and said, "This is ridiculous . . . I'm leaving."

As the student walked toward the door, the professor bolted up to confront him. "You can't leave my classroom."

"Oh, yes I can," replied the student, "just watch me."

"Okay, okay," said the professor, "but before you leave, you must tell me your name. I do not believe I know your name."

The frustration on the student's face turned quickly to a grin. He reached down, grabbed his foot with one hand and pointed at it with the other, all the while staring at the professor.

"You tell me what my name is, sir. You tell me."

alternative fishing areas in the backwaters are frozen and eagles concentrate along the main channel," notes Henry Schneider of the refuge. The city of Wabasha, Minnesota, has an observation deck staffed with Eagle Watch volunteers on weekends from November until March. Call the Winona, Minnesota, Convention and Visitors Bureau at (800) 657-4972 for more information on eagle and swan watch tours.

Staging

A magnificent birding time is during staging, when large flocks of migrating birds gather in a concentrated area to feed, rest, or wait out bad weather. Places like Cape May in New Jersey and Fisherman Island National Wildlife Refuge, Virginia, can offer phenomenal viewing of staging birds. Fisherman Island has hosted millions of passerines such as eastern bluebirds, eastern meadowlarks, and tree swallows during fall migration. In November at Riecks Lake Park, north of Alma, Wisconsin, tundra swans stage until freeze-up before continuing their journey to the East Coast.

STEP THREE: DEVELOP WILDLIFE VIEWING SKILLS AND TECHNIQUES

Wildlife is often closer and more abundant than you might think. Developing sharp senses is the first step to seeing more animals in the field. While looking for wildlife, make it a game to really focus your eyes and tune your ears. Most animals camouflage themselves, blending into the environment, so you'll need to look at more than the obvious. Try the following:

■ Look for subtle movements in bushes, shrubs, and trees.

■ Make "owl eyes"—make an "okay" sign with your hand, bring the rest of your fingers into the circle, then look through them. This helps focus your attention.

■ Look for parts of an animal, rather than its entire body.

Some additional suggestions from the National Partners in Watchable Wildlife brochure, "Ultimate Guide to Wildlife Watching," include:

■ Make "mule ears"—cup your hands over your ears to amplify natural sounds.

■ Look above and below you. Animals occupy niches in all the vertical and horizontal layers of a habitat. Don't just look directly in front of you; look up and down, too.

■ Heed your instincts. If the hair on the back of your neck stands up, an animal may be near.

■ Relax your muscles. Animals can easily detect tension.

■ Look for out-of-place shapes, such as horizontal shapes in a mostly vertical forest, or an oblong shape on a linear tree branch.

■ Focus and expand your attention, taking in the foreground and then switching to take in the wide view.

■ Use your peripheral vision rather than turning your head.

The animal you are watching most likely considers you a predator. Take yourself out of that role. The following tricks can help:

■ Avoid sudden movements. Many animals will tolerate observation if no quick motions or loud noises are made.

■ Do not try to sneak up on animals. It probably won't work and you may place yourself in danger.

■ Do not stare at animals. Wear a hat that conceals your eyes.

Strategies

Use these strategies to get close to wildlife:

■ Use optics.
■ Use a vehicle as a blind.
■ Hide behind a blind.
■ Sit still.
■ Walk quietly and slowly.
■ Place decoys.
■ Mask or wear scents.
■ Set bait.

■ Imitate calls.
■ Use special lights.
■ Hire a professional guide.
■ Go on guided outings.

Optics

As already noted, using binoculars and spotting scopes are the two best ways to get close to wildlife. (See page 41 for more on selecting and using optics.)

Using a Vehicle as a Blind

Vehicles make excellent blinds, even though this method is certainly not as cool or as glitzy as other wildlife viewing techniques. Many animals have become habituated to vehicles; they don't seem to be afraid of them and will often approach or pass right by your car. Turn your engine off, sit quietly in your vehicle and wait for wildlife to come to you. If you need to shift around inside your vehicle, move slowly. Do not get out when animals are near—you'll send them off in an acute panic. If you see animals while your car is running, don't turn the engine off, since this will also panic them.

Blinds

A blind is anything that conceals you from the animals you want to observe. Blinds may include your vehicle, boxes, homemade blinds, even fancy, portable, commercial blinds similar to a pop-up tent. Some modern blinds actually roll out over your body from a helmet, popping over you from a backpacklike frame.

Blinds are used because some animals, such as waterfowl, have excellent eyesight, and blinds conceal your movement. Place blinds upwind, and have the sun to your back, so the animal will have to look into the sun in order to see you. Don't set up blinds in the midst of wildlife. Blinds do not give you the right to get too close.

The Medicine Lake National Wildlife Refuge in Medicine Lake, Montana, provides a sharp-tailed grouse photo blind that can be reserved on a first-come, first-served basis. The blind is erected near a busy dancing ground in mid-April and is removed once the grouse have completed their breeding displays, according to Robert Romero, refuge operations specialist. From the blind, photographers and wildlife viewers are treated to a view of the elaborate courtship ritual—strutting and stomping—of male sharp-tailed grouse. To reserve the blind, contact Medicine Lake National Wildlife Refuge, 223 North Lake Shore Road, Medicine Lake, MT 59247-9600; phone (406) 789-2305.

Lostwood National Wildlife Refuge also maintains a blind for watching male grouse attempt to woo their females, and boasts one of the highest populations of sharp-tailed grouse in the nation. Contact Lostwood National Wildlife Refuge, Rural Route 2, Box 98, Kenmare, ND 58746; phone (701) 848-2722.

Sitting Still

Find a comfortable place, sit down, relax, and remain still. Most animals' eyes are made to detect motion. Lean up against a tree to break your silhouette. Trees and vegetation make great viewing blinds. If you wear dark-colored clothes or camouflage and use a dropcloth of camouflage netting, you'll increase the odds of going unnoticed. If you sit absolutely still, you will also see animals reappear because they'll think you have gone.

Sitting aloof may also help. Act disinterested. Look around slowly and not directly at animals.

wind direction

Walk Quietly and Slowly

Few animals walk with the steady gait that humans do. Break your natural pattern: take a few steps, avoiding brittle sticks or leaves, then stop, look, and listen.

Walk into the wind whenever possible, since many animals have an excellent sense of smell (see illustration on opposite page). Bob Hernbrode of the Colorado Division of Wildlife suggests that if you cross rivers or streams, you should "look upstream and downstream. Often the sound of the flowing water will deaden your noise and the animal will not realize you are close." Or take a roundabout route, and consider your silhouette.

Do not approach any animal directly—act disinterested. Look all around you, and again, do not stare at the animal. If that bird or deer you are moving toward appears nervous or skittish, stop until it feels comfortable. If you begin to approach again and the animal still appears nervous or skittish, you are too close. From here, break out your binoculars and watch from the distance where the animal is comfortable.

How close is too close? In Yellowstone National Park, approaching on foot within one hundred yards of any wildlife—or within any distance that disturbs or displaces wildlife—is strictly prohibited.

Decoys

According to archeological research, Native Americans used decoys more than two thousand years ago, crafting them from tule reeds, cattails, twine, feathers, and mineral paint. A decoy lures an animal within range for a better view or photograph. To wild animals, decoys represent companionship and safety, and point to a feeding and resting area.

Decoys are often used in conjunction with blinds. Some successful waterfowl decoys are much, much larger than real birds. And hunters have discovered that decoys need not be lifelike. Snow geese, for example, will decoy to pieces of sheet or white plastic bleach bottles.

Decoys have been used to lure ducks, geese, shorebirds, pronghorn antelope, deer, elk, sandhill cranes, blue herons, and wild turkeys. Some seasoned wildlife watchers place a heron or crane silhouette near their blinds as a "confidence builder" for other species; the sight of these long-legged, wary birds can convince ducks or geese that an area is safe.

Positioning decoys is an art, as any waterfowl hunter will tell you. For example, relaxed ducks that are feeding tend to spread themselves out. If your decoys are all bunched up, real ducks may interpret them as a nervous flock about to depart.

Scents

There are two types of scents: attracting scents and cover scents.

Attracting scents pull animals to you. These scents include such aromatic delicacies as urine of fox, rabbit, deer, or elk, as well as apples, bacon drippings, or fish. Place these upwind of your blind.

Cover scents mask your scent. Bob Hernbrode explains that cover scents are usually placed a few feet or yards downwind from a blind. "Skunk is the most common and effective of these cover scents," he says, "although others such as apples or sage are also used. Scents are usually applied to a cotton ball hung from a string, or placed on the ground—they may also be used on your person, on a sleeve, hat, or shoes, to cover your own scent as you move around."

Baiting

Baiting is the use of food to attract wildlife. Although a few wildlife watchers use baiting, most wildlife professionals do not support the practice. It is highly artificial as well as strictly regulated in many areas. Limit baiting to your backyard birdfeeder.

Calls

Many animals can be "called in" with the use of sounds. Coyotes, foxes, bobcats, squirrels, deer, elk, moose, antelope, pheasants, wild turkeys, waterfowl, and many songbirds will respond to calls. To make a wildlife call, do the following:

■ Loudly whisper "psh" or "hiss" into your hand. This will call in songbirds such as nuthatches and chickadees.

■ Kiss the back of your hand to create a higher-pitched squealing sound. This will bring in many birds and small mammals.

■ Rattle deer or elk antlers on a fall afternoon. This can attract rutting deer.

■ Play tape recordings of animal sounds. The recorded squeals of a dying rabbit can bring in owls.

Calling animals with recordings is controversial. Limit calls to common species; use calls only during times of the year when it will not distress the animal. Never use calls or recordings for rare or endangered species of wildlife. Taped calls are prohibited in many areas, so check with the site manager before you use calls. When in doubt, don't.

Montana forester and photographer Bill Gabriel notes that in some areas, tape recorders can be detrimental to wildlife. "People playing recordings under a nesting tree caused some common black hawks to abandon the Sonoita Creek Sanctuary in Arizona, and some of the few elegant trogons in the United States were harassed out of Arizona's Cave Creek Canyon by people with tape players." Bill offers the following dos and don'ts for using a tape recorder:

■ DO take time to learn the songs and call notes of the species you are interested in pursuing.

■ DON'T use territorial songs unless you first hear a singing bird.

■ DO play the call only a few times. If no bird responds, move on and try another area.

■ DO turn off the tape as soon as the bird responds.

■ DON'T use tapes in areas where few people visit a few special birds.

■ DO keep the volume at a minimum. More is not better.

DIFFERENCES? WHAT DIFFERENCES?

While I was a graduate student at Yale, I had the opportunity to study under Dr. Stephen Kellert, world-renowned for his pioneering work in understanding public attitudes toward wildlife. After graduating, I started my career as a wildlife biologist with the Florida Game and Fresh Water Fish Commission. One of my first assignments was a public speaking engagement with a raccoon hunting club in north Florida.

Eager to share what I had learned while working with Dr. Kellert, I talked about public attitudes toward wildlife. I asserted that when it comes to people and their views of wildlife, there is no such thing as a "general public." People who live in rural areas think about wildlife differently than people who live in urban or suburban areas, I said. Older citizens think differently about wildlife than do people who are twenty-five to forty years old. Women think differently than men.

A rather large raccoon hunter stood up in the back of the room, totally unimpressed with my lecture thus far. "Boy, are you married?" he asked.

"Yes sir," I replied cautiously, wondering where this was leading.

He continued, "Well, it doesn't take no research project from Yale to tell me that men and women think differently, now, does it?"

Lights

Many animals cannot see red light; to them, it just looks black. Some wildlife watchers use red beams in conjunction with blinds at night to view nocturnal creatures.

Hiring a Guide

Don't be afraid to look for experienced hunting or fishing guides to help you make the most of a wildlife viewing trip. More and more hunting and fishing guides are being hired by wildlife viewers. Guides know the area and the tricks of the trade, such as how to place decoys, call in turkeys and ducks, and find wildlife.

On Maryland's Eastern Shore, traditional waterfowl hunting guides take out more and more wildlife watchers each year. Though guides are expensive, their expertise is usually worth the money. With a guide, it's possible to learn in an afternoon what would take you a month or more to figure out on your own.

Guided Outings

Most parks and refuges offer nature and wildlife walks, and many local Audubon groups and other wildlife organizations offer outings guided by professionals. There's no better way to learn about wildlife than from people who have made wildlife management their profession.

STEP FOUR: UNDERSTAND THE SPECIES AND ITS HABITS

When viewing an animal, observe its colors, shape, "field marks," and behavior. Hone your skills in identifying different species, and notice the differences between male and female animals, and between younger animals and older ones. For example, although the Kentucky warbler and the common yellowthroat look somewhat similar, the Kentucky warbler has distinctive yellow patches, like spectacles, around its eyes. Female belted kingfishers have brown breastbands while males do not. Juvenile bald eagles lack the distinctive white head and tail so characteristic of adult birds.

Wildlife Identification

Identifying wildlife is a lifelong process. Nothing will help you more than a good set of field guides to go with your binoculars. Start off by identifying the animal as a mammal, bird, fish, reptile, amphibian, or insect. Then ask yourself the following questions:

What is the animal's size?
Size makes a difference. Beavers and muskrats are both aquatic

mammals, but once you learn a few key characteristics you can easily tell one from the other. The beaver has a broad, hairless, paddle-shaped tail; the muskrat's tail is thin and ropelike. Beavers grow much larger than muskrats. An adult beaver weighs between thirty and sixty pounds, while an adult muskrat weighs between two and four pounds.

What is the animal's color?

Color helps distinguish between species and between sexes. Male ducks, known as *drakes*, are brightly colored in the spring. Some animals change color for winter, such as the snowshoe or varying hare. Short-tailed weasels shed brown summer coats for white winter ones. The white-tailed ptarmigan, found in some mountainous areas of the West, changes its plumage from pure white in winter to a mottled gray, brown, and white in summer.

What is the animal's shape?

Observe the beak of a red-tailed hawk. It's hooked and stout and perfect for tearing flesh. Now notice the bill of a blue-winged teal. It's flat and fairly long, and is used to strain tiny animals from the water. Paying attention to the shape of an animal's features can help in identification. For instance, white-tailed deer antlers have a main

beam with tines branching from it; a mule deer's antlers branch more uniformly. Bald and golden eagles fly with flattened wings, unlike vultures, which soar with their wings in a "V," and ospreys, which fly with wings that appear bent.

What type of habitat is the animal in?

The red fox prefers open fields, meadows, and edge habitats whereas the gray fox prefers more wooded areas, as illustrated below.

Is the animal vocalizing?

Green tree frogs "queenk," southern leopard frogs give three to five "croaks" followed by two or three "clucks," and bullfrogs call "jug-o'-rum." Great horned owls hoot, "Hoo, hoo-oo, hoo, hoo"; barred owls call, "Hoohoo-hoohoo, hoohoo-hoohooaw"; and great gray owls sing, "Whoo-hoo-hoo."

What is the animal doing?

Specific activities can often give important clues for identification. Dabbling ducks feed by doing a sort of headstand, tipping their rumps in the air as they probe for grasses and the seeds of underwater plants. Dabbling ducks can take flight from the water directly into the air.

EXPERIENCED SNAKE HANDLER; DON'T TRY THIS AT HOME

While living in Tallahassee, Florida, I had the opportunity to take a field ecology course at Florida State University with one of the best field biologists in the nation, Dr. Bruce Means. Dr. Means seems to be an authority on every animal that moves, but he is renowned for his work with rattlesnakes.

On one of many field trips, our class took a respite from the midday Florida sun and went swimming in a cool, crystalline spring in Apalachicola National Forest. Quite hungry after swimming, we began hiking back to the van for lunch, stepping more quickly as we became hungrier and hungrier.

I took off running, yelling to my teacher that I would beat him back to the van. Pounding along the fire road, I leaped over a large branch. Only in midair did I realize that it wasn't a branch at all, but the largest eastern diamondback rattlesnake I had ever seen, stretched completely across the road, sunning itself. I caught my footing and turned to warn the others.

Any sane individual, upon seeing this five-foot-long reptile, would have stepped back in amazement. But, without hesitation, and clad only in his swimsuit, Dr. Means reached down with both hands and PICKED UP THE SNAKE. Johnny Weissmuller's Tarzan movies may have been filmed at Wakulla Springs, not ten miles away, but I was witnessing a real-life Tarzan! So much for the professor in the ivory tower. This was real-world Biology 101.

One by one we examined the monstrous rattlesnake writhing in our professor's hands. Then Dr. Means walked calmly over to the side of the fire road and released it. "Wouldn't want anyone to step on him," he commented, quickly adding, "Class dismissed."

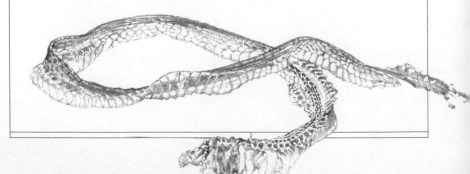

Diving or sea ducks dive completely underwater to feed on small fish, crustaceans, mollusks, and aquatic plants. These ducks must run or patter along the top of the water to build up speed before taking flight.

Is the animal found in this region? This habitat?

Once you are reasonably sure you have identified the animal you are watching, consult your field guide's section on the species' range and habitat to make sure it lives in the area in which you have found it.

Animal Behavior

Don't just look at wildlife—learn to observe it. What is the animal doing? Resting? Feeding? Try to understand what you are seeing and hearing. What might look like random behavior is actually the animal performing an important survival function. Here are some examples:

■ Shorebirds use their bills to "feel" for food. Highly sensitive and specialized nerve endings in their bills enable shorebirds to seize crustaceans in the sand. Watch them probe for snails, clams, and worms. Observe how the different bill lengths are related to the foods each species eats.

■ The yellow-bellied sapsucker pokes holes around the trunk of a tree, not to eat animals in the bark but to allow sap to ooze out. Insects become stranded in the sap, providing this resourceful bird with a meal.

■ In Badlands National Park, visitors often wonder why bison take dust baths in the loose dirt of prairie dog towns. The coating of dust helps protect bison from pesky insects.

Wildlife Calling Cards: Tracks and Signs

You don't always have to see wildlife to enjoy wildlife. Animals often leave clues about their movements and daily routines. Among these are the following:

77

TRACK TRAPS

*T*ry "trapping" tracks by smoothing over sand or mud (preferably near water) and returning the next day to see what may have walked by. The tracks shown here belong to deer.

■ Owl pellets. Owls cannot digest the fur and bones of the small mammals they eat. These lovely leftovers are regurgitated in pellet form. Look for them around the bases of large trees. If you find pellets, you're probably standing beneath an owl's home base.

■ Whitewash. Look for "whitewash" (droppings) on cliffs or beneath trees. This indicates the presence of a roost, nest, or colony of birds.

■ Game trails. These narrow trails mark routes to food, shelter, or water.

■ Fur/hair. You may find fur or hair along the edges of the entrance to a den tree or on a fence where animals have passed. Inspect the fur. What color is it?

■ Deer rubs. Look for marks on trees from antler rubbing or gnawing.

■ Dead birds. These are often the remains of a predator's meal.

■ Browse lines. Look for leafless areas in shrubs and stands of young trees. These are caused by too many feeding deer in an area.

■ Woodpecker signs. Rows of small holes encircling live trees are signs of yellow-bellied sapsuckers.

■ Bird nests. Nests come in all shapes and sizes. Early spring, prior to green-up, is a great time to see and inspect nests of previous years. Can you associate a particular nest with the bird that made it?

■ Flattened grass. Tamped grass in a field or clearing tells you that an animal has bedded down there.

■ Scat—okay, animal poop. Scat can be identified by its contents. Black bear scat is soft and dark in the fall but resembles horse manure in summer. Mountain lion scat looks like large domestic cat scat.

■ Rises. When trout and other fish species feed in a lake or stream, they make small dimples, or rises, on the surface of the water as they tip upward to eat insects or other aquatic life.

■ Tracks. Look for animal tracks in snow, in loose dirt, in soft ground, or near water. Bears, skunks, beavers, porcupines, and raccoons walk flatfooted. Wolves, foxes, coyotes, mountain lions, and bobcats walk on their toes. Deer, elk, moose, pronghorn, mountain sheep, and mountain goats walk on their toenails or hooves.

■ Shoreline clues. Notice stick and mud dams across streams; large conical houses of mud and sticks at the edge of a lake; pointed tree stumps near water. Any or all of these signs will tell you that beavers live in the area.

■ Sounds. Listen for the characteristic "slap" of water as a beaver dives below the surface; the sound is made by the beaver's tail striking the water and serves as a warning for others of potential danger.

Wildlife Management

Most of the wildlife you view lives partly as the result of work by wildlife management professionals. While in the field, you may notice some of the following management techniques:

Water Control

On many national wildlife refuges and state waterfowl-wetland management areas, water control is one of the most important management tools. Managers construct dikes and create shallow impoundments for wildlife. Water in marshes is drained in spring, stimulating plant growth and thus providing food for ducks and geese. In fall, marshes are flooded again to make seeds available to waterfowl. At Trustom Pond Refuge in Rhode Island, wildlife managers lower water levels by opening breachways to the ocean. This practice exposes mudflats, which become feeding areas for shorebirds and nesting islands for common terns.

Controlled Burning

Periodic regulated burning of many ecosystems, including grasslands and some forests, is essential for maintaining productive wildlife habitat. In the Florida Keys, the U.S. Fish and Wildlife Service burns woody undergrowth. This stimulates the growth of tender shoots, providing food for the diminutive Key deer. In Congaree Swamp National Monument in South Carolina, park managers set prescribed burns to maintain critical nesting habitat for the federally listed endangered red-cockaded woodpecker.

Nest Boxes and Platforms

Nest boxes are common sights in wildlife viewing areas. Placed along field edges, small nest boxes are designed to attract bluebirds and provide homes where there is a shortage of natural cavities. These boxes are usually about five feet above ground and have an entrance hole that is one-half to one inch in diameter. Larger wood duck boxes are placed in wetland areas. Metal guards are placed below these boxes to keep out predators such as raccoons and snakes.

Nesting platforms for ospreys are generally built eight to ten feet (or higher) above open water. Nesting platforms for Canada geese are only a foot or two above open shallow water or on the edge of a marsh.

Plantings

In the prairie pothole region, wildlife managers plant native grasses to provide nesting cover for waterfowl. At Eufaula National Wildlife Refuge in Alabama, they plant large tracts of winter grain, such as soybeans, peanuts, millet, corn, and sorghum. These crops are used by waterfowl during winter.

Seasonal Closures

Many parks and refuges close certain areas to visitors to protect sensitive wildlife during critical times of the year. In winter, wildlife managers in the West close certain trails to snowmobilers to protect mule deer and elk; these animals are already stressed due to limited availability of forage. Shorebirds are particularly sensitive to human intrusion while nesting, so prohibiting entry to shorebird nesting areas is critical for nesting success.

Fortunately, most people agree with this wildlife management practice. In a public opinion study I conducted for the Georgia Wildlife Resources Division, 86 percent of respondents moderately or strongly supported limiting public access to certain fish and wildlife management areas to protect sensitive wildlife.

Law Enforcement

Wildlife managers must also enforce the law. Law enforcement is an important management tool, since it curbs poaching and fosters appropriate interactions with wildlife.

It's also a dangerous part of the job. My consulting work has taken me to nearly every state fish and wildlife agency in the nation at one time or another; I don't know of one office that does not have a plaque on its walls memorializing a wildlife officer killed in the line of duty.

Wildlife Population Monitoring

At a viewing site, you might get lucky and see biologists banding, trapping, or releasing wild animals. Bird banding and census-taking of wildlife populations are two methods employed by biologists to measure the health of animal populations.

Mowing

Mown areas on refuges or in wildlife management areas maintain open habitat for wildlife such as the American woodcock, bobwhite quail, and whitetail deer.

FEELING LUCKY? NOT SO FAMOUS BEAR STORIES

One of the thrills of wildlife watching is that you can never be sure exactly when you will see wildlife. Sometimes it takes days to see what you are after. Other times wildlife reveals itself unexpectedly. Be prepared for both.

As a high school student I spent many weekends backpacking in Shenandoah National Park with Jim Omans, now a forester with the Department of Defense. One exceptionally dark night we set up camp in White Oak Canyon, a beautiful gorge noted for its many waterfalls and virgin hemlock stands.

In the middle of the night I was awakened by a ripping sound—the sound of a raccoon ripping up my brand-new backpack. It seemed strange that a raccoon would be able to reach our packs, since Jim and I had hung them from a tree to elude the many marauding black bears in the area. Clad only in underwear and untied hiking boots, I went over to shoo the raccoon away.

Stumbling through pitch darkness toward the sound of continuous ripping, I reached the packs and was surprised at how low they were now hanging. "Oh well," I said to myself, "my knot must have slipped." I began to shove at the pack, believing the raccoon would startle and run for cover. This particular raccoon seemed to be quite large, probably due to all the free lunches it was getting from campers. But I wasn't deterred; it wasn't going to get any more of my food.

I pushed again. Then my flashlight slipped and the beam illuminated the ground, where a very large raccoon labored on, shredding my pack—only I saw now that it wasn't a raccoon at all, but a fairly large black bear, now face-to-face with me!

I pushed myself back, stumbling to the ground. Jim came over and we began yelling to scare the bear away. But the bear

➤ showed little concern over a future wildlife biologist and a forester in their underwear and untied hiking boots. It continued to enjoy a freeze-dried beef stroganoff dinner.

This was not the last of my unexpected bouts with bears. Shortly after I was married, my wife Mary Anne and I journeyed to the Great Smoky Mountains National Park to hike and view wildlife. I was well-acquainted with the park, having worked there for two summers as a teenager, and I knew one of the best places in the park to see bears was Mount LeConte. Citing many facts on black bear ecology and biology, I impressed my bride with my knowledge of bears. Except—the bears never showed.

After a long day of hiking we set up for a snack on a rocky outcropping atop Mount LeConte, complete with a 150-foot cliff and a spectacular view. We were enjoying the scenery when Mary Anne caught sight of a black bear. "Keep still," I said, "we'll get a better view."

A better view we did get, as the bear ambled slowly toward us. Pleased with our good luck, I glanced back out over the cliff to enjoy the view. Then it hit me: we were sandwiched between a 250-pound bear and a 150-foot cliff. My wife, confident of the situation—she was accompanied by a bear expert after all—enjoyed the experience, even remarking, "Here we are with a cliff behind us and a bear in front of us."

"Yeah," I slowly replied.

Luckily the bear lost interest in us and soon left the area (as I'd predicted he would).

Encountering the animals you set out to see can be a real challenge. Before a trip to Denali National Park in Alaska, I had never observed a grizzly bear in the wild. Thrilled at the possibility, I made plans and collected information. "What time of day is best to see grizzlies?" I asked. "What areas are best to see one? Have any grizzlies been spotted within the past few days?" After several unsuccessful forays into the park, I came to the disappointing conclusion that I would have to wait to see a grizzly.

The day of our departure, I decided to try one last time. ➤

"The train back to Anchorage won't wait for us," my wife reminded me. But I had to try again. It might be several years before I returned. I spent several hours touring an area known to have occasional grizzly sightings. Again I was disappointed, and found little consolation in the wise words I had often given to novice viewers—the theory that so much wildlife viewing happens by chance.

And then chance paid me a visit. Seemingly out of nowhere, a very blonde, very large grizzly appeared, walking slowly up a streambed. My first thought was that my wife would not believe me when I told her—she had accompanied me on my previous excursions. My second thought was that, for the first time during the trip, I did not have my camera at my side. But there it was.

The female bear, called a sow, walked slowly up the streambed in plain view three hundred yards away. I noted the distinct hump above her shoulders, her very large size, and her coloration; she was so blonde she was nearly pale yellow. I followed her through my binoculars for close to fifteen minutes, savoring the view and my good fortune. Then I quickly traveled back to the lodge where my wife and daughter were in line for the shuttle bus and anxiously awaiting my return. Luckily, the bus was late, and I was able to catch the train back to Anchorage.

5 | Fifteen Great Wildlife Viewing Trips

You don't have to travel halfway across the country for great wildlife viewing. Chances are, you'll find excellent viewing just a few miles from home. Nevertheless, there are several places in the United States that stand out as world-class wildlife viewing sites. Here's a list of some of my favorites.

Bighorn sheep, Georgetown Viewing Site, Georgetown, Colorado

Located along Interstate 70, approximately halfway between the cities of Denver and Vail, the Georgetown Viewing Site is among the most accessible places in the nation for viewing Rocky Mountain bighorn sheep. Between 175 and 200 bighorns occupy the rocky cliffs along the north side of Clear Creek Canyon. Fall and winter are the

best times to view or see them. Wildlife managers have constructed a tower shaped like a ram's horn from which people may view the sheep; the exhibit includes interpretive displays and mounted viewing scopes. Look closely; the sheep blend well with the terrain.

For more information, contact the Colorado Division of Wildlife, 6060 Broadway, Denver, CO 80216; phone (303) 297-1192. Be sure to purchase a copy of the division's *Bighorn Sheep Watching* guide for $3.

Alaskan brown bears, McNeil River State Game Sanctuary, Alaska

On the shores along Mifkik Creek and McNeil River Falls at the McNeil River State Game Sanctuary, Alaskan brown bears congregate to fish for migrating salmon. You'll see two to fifteen bears feeding here when the salmon run is on. Only ten people per day are allowed into the sanctuary to avoid disturbing the bears.

In June, viewing opportunities are at Mifkik Creek; the action moves to McNeil Falls in July and August with still more bears. Because of the extreme popularity of this viewing site, the Alaska Department of Fish and Game holds a lottery to select among hundreds of applicants.

Applications to the Alaska Department of Fish and Game must be postmarked no later than March 1 and arrive by March 15 of every year. Such a spectacular opportunity has its price: a $20 nonrefundable application fee, and a user fee if you are selected ($100 for Alaska residents and $250 for nonresidents). Access to the site is by floatplane, which costs about $300 to charter. There are no facilities, so you must camp, and there is a four-mile-round-trip hike to the falls. Bringing children is not recommended.

To apply for this viewing chance of a lifetime, write the Alaska Department of Fish and Game, Wildlife Division, 333 Raspberry Road, Anchorage, AK 99518-1599; phone (907) 267-2179.

Manatees, Crystal River National Wildlife Refuge, Florida

The gentle, slow-moving endangered Florida manatee is a large aquatic mammal, typically ten feet long and weighing a thousand pounds. Manatees live in shallow, slow rivers, river mouths, estuaries, saltwater bays, and shallow coastal areas. In the United States, manatees have been found as far north as Virginia in summer; during winter, especially in cold weather, they congregate in warm-water discharges from power plants and warm springs, such as those found in Kings Bay, part of the Crystal River National Wildlife Refuge.

In recent years, more than two hundred manatees have used the Kings Bay area as wintering grounds. The bay offers unparalleled opportunities for viewing these gentle giants. Contact Crystal River National Wildlife Refuge, 1502 Southeast Kings Bay Drive, Crystal River, FL 34429; phone (904) 563-2088.

Rocky Mountain elk, Horseshoe Park, Rocky Mountain National Park, Colorado

During September and October, bull elk bugle as a physical release and to challenge other males during the fall rut. Listening to the bugle of an elk on a clear, crisp evening in the Rocky Mountains is an experience you will never forget. Bugling usually begins an hour before sunset and starts off as a low, hollow sound, rising to a high-pitched shriek, and culminating in a series of grunts.

One of the most reliable places to hear elk bugling in the fall is Horseshoe Park in Rocky Mountain National Park. Contact Rocky

Mountain National Park, Estes Park, CO 80517; phone (303) 586-1206.

Sandhill cranes, Platte River, Nebraska

For about five weeks in early spring (March), more than three-quarters of the world's population of sandhill cranes gathers along the Platte River in central Nebraska. You'll see more than 500,000 of these stately birds, resting and fattening up as they migrate back to breeding grounds in the Arctic.

The local chamber of commerce sponsors a three-day program/celebration (usually during the second weekend in March) known as "Wings over the Platte." Bus tours, viewing blinds, guided field trips, seminars, workshops, and wildlife art exhibits are featured. Contact Field Supervisor, U.S. Fish and Wildlife Service, 203 West Second Street, Grand Island, NE 68801; phone (308) 382-6468. Or contact Grand Island/Hall County Convention and Visitors Bureau at (800) 658-3178. Make hotel reservations well in advance.

California and Steller's sea lions, Sea Lion Caves, Oregon

Here, you will enter another world. After descending more than two hundred feet in an elevator to Sea Lion Caves on the coast of Oregon, you will find dim light, the hollow sound of waves crashing against cliffs, and the echoed barks of hundreds of Steller's sea lions (present year-round) and California sea lions (present from September to April). Sea lions swim and loaf below a cliff-top observation deck. Contact Sea Lion Caves, 91560 U.S. Highway 101, Florence, OR 97439; phone (503) 547-3111.

Gray whales, Channel Islands National Marine Sanctuary, California

The annual wintertime migration of the endangered gray whale brings these giant cetaceans directly off the coast of Southern California. Watching a gray whale thrust its fifty-foot-long body out of the water, rotate in midair, and crash back to the ocean will make your heart pound just a little bit faster. Some of the best whale-watching takes place aboard commercial boats that offer trips. But there are also good viewing opportunities from shore at the many points in the area: Point Conception, north of Santa Barbara; Point Dume in Malibu; and Point Loma in San Diego. In Ventura Harbor, visit the Channel Islands National Park Visitor Center: you'll find a viewing tower complete with spotting scopes for watching whales. Whales can be seen from December through April. Contact Channel Islands National Marine Sanctuary, 113 Harbor Way, Santa Barbara, CA 93109; phone (805) 966-7107.

For whale-watching boat trips contact the following:

- Bay Queen Harbor Cruises, 1691 Spinnaker Drive, Ventura Harbor, CA 93001; phone (805) 642-7753
- Island Packers, Inc., 1867 Spinnaker Drive, Ventura Harbor, CA 93001; phone (805) 642-1393
- Bailey's Tophat Charter, c/o Cisco's, Channel Islands Harbor, CA; phone (805) 985-8511
- Marina Sailing, 3600 South Harbor Boulevard, Channel Islands Harbor, CA; phone (805) 985-5219

Birds at Cape May, New Jersey

World-famous for its birding opportunities and ornithological research, Cape May, New Jersey, is considered one of the best birding sites in the world. From the southern tip of New Jersey, Cape May juts into Delaware Bay. Migrating birds are funneled here by geography; they stop to rest before making the eighteen-mile cross-bay flight.

More than four hundred species of birds have been recorded in the Cape May region. Large numbers of raptors (hawks, falcons, eagles) are regularly seen during fall migrations, as are songbirds (almost one hundred species). Visit the Cape May Bird Observatory, funded by the New Jersey Audubon Society, Box 3, Cape May Point, NJ 08212; phone (609) 884-2736.

J. N. "Ding" Darling National Wildlife Refuge, Florida

Boasting almost three hundred species of birds, more than fifty species of reptiles and amphibians, and more than thirty different species of mammals, "Ding" Darling National Wildlife Refuge is one of the most popular wildlife refuges in the nation. The refuge is located on Sanibel Island in southwest Florida. The site's five-mile, one-way auto tour offers excellent viewing. Plan to be at the observation tower at sunset in hopes of seeing roseate spoonbills flying overhead.

This refuge was named to commemorate Jay Norwood Darling, a pioneer in wildlife conservation. Darling's distinguished career included serving as head of the U.S. Biological Survey, forerunner of the U.S. Fish and Wildlife Service. He also initiated the Duck Stamp (Migratory Bird Hunting Stamp) and was a key figure in the establishment of the National Wildlife Refuge System. He won Pulitzer Prizes in 1923 and 1942 for his satirical conservation and political cartoons. Contact J.N. Ding Darling National Wildlife Refuge, 1 Wildlife Drive, Sanibel, FL 33957; phone (813) 472-1100.

Kirtland's warbler, Michigan

Six inches long, the endangered Kirtland's warbler is considered a large warbler. After wintering in the Bahamas, this bird returns each spring to a six-county area of Michigan's northern Lower Peninsula—the only place in the world where it nests. Fewer than six hundred breeding pairs of Kirtland's warblers exist, so viewing this rare, beautiful warbler is a thrill never to be forgotten.

The U.S. Fish and Wildlife Service and the Michigan Department of Natural Resources provide free daily tours of warbler habitat during May and June out of Grayling, Michigan. Contact U.S. Fish and Wildlife Service, Ecological Services Office, 1405 South Harrison Road, Room 302, East Lansing, MI 48823; phone (517) 337-6650. The USDA Forest Service provides daily tours out of Mio, Michigan; phone (517) 826-3252 for more information. If you want to head out on your own, drive the forty-eight-mile Jack Pine Wildlife Viewing Tour, beginning in Mio. Contact the Michigan Department of Natural Resources at (517) 826-3211.

Hawk Mountain Sanctuary, Pennsylvania

Migrating from breeding grounds in the northeastern United States and eastern Canada to wintering grounds in the southeastern United States, Mexico, and Central and South America, thousands of raptors pass over the rocky outcroppings of Hawk Mountain Sanctuary on Pennsylvania's Kittatinny Ridge during September and October.

Fourteen species routinely cross this ridge along the eastern flyway, including broad-winged hawks, sharp-shinned hawks, Cooper's hawks, bald eagles, and ospreys. Hawk Mountain regulars say the best viewing is usually between September 10 and September 25. Contact Hawk Mountain Sanctuary, Route 2, Kempton, PA 19529; phone (610) 756-6961.

Mexican free-tailed bats, Carlsbad Caverns National Park, New Mexico

On warm summer evenings in the Chihuahuan Desert, thousands of Mexican free-tailed bats exit in a whirling, smokelike column from the natural mouth of Carlsbad Caverns. An estimated 300,000 bats inhabit the caverns; they emerge at dusk to feed on moths and other night-flying insects, returning to the caverns before dawn. The best flights occur in late August and September, when young bats born in June join the evening ritual.

Bat Flight Amphitheater, located at the mouth of the cavern, seats up to a thousand people. Rangers give programs about the bats from Memorial Day to Labor Day prior to the evening flights. But don't expect to see bats if you visit in winter—they'll have migrated to Mexico. Contact Carlsbad Caverns National Park, 3225 National Parks Highway, Carlsbad, NM 88220; phone (505) 785-2232.

Bald eagles, Skagit River, Washington

One of the largest concentrations of wintering bald eagles in the lower forty-eight states occurs at the Skagit River Bald Eagle Natural Area in northern Washington State. More than three hundred bald eagles gather along the Skagit River to feed on spawned-out chum salmon, feeding along gravel bars between 7 A.M. and 11 A.M. Eagles feed here between November and early March, with peak numbers in mid-January. Contact The Nature Conservancy, Washington Field Office, 217 Pine Street, No. 1100, Seattle, WA 98101; phone (206) 343-4344. Or contact Mount Baker Ranger District, 2105 Highway 20, Sedro Woolley, WA 98284; phone (360) 856-5700. Also contact Washington Department of Wildlife, Region 4, Nongame Program, 16018 Mill Creek Boulevard, Mill Creek, WA 98012; phone (206) 775-1311.

Wintering elk, National Elk Refuge, Wyoming

Elk gather in one of the largest winter concentrations in the United States at the National Elk Refuge in Jackson, Wyoming. When snow comes to the high country in the region, elk migrate from high-elevation summer range to winter range in the valley. Almost 7,500 elk inhabit the area, staging America's version of an African plains scene, with thousands of animals stretched across the valley. Elk arrive in early November and return to the high country in early May.

In winter, visitors can view elk from a horse-drawn sleigh. Sleighs run from late December to March, 10 A.M. to 4 P.M. daily. Tours operate from the National Wildlife Art Museum, three miles north of Jackson on U.S. Highway 26/191. Contact the National Elk Refuge, 675 East Broadway, P.O. Box C, Jackson, WY 83001; phone (307) 733-9212.

Lesser prairie chickens, Comanche National Grassland, Colorado

With rapid, stomping feet, dropped wings, and raised neck feathers, the male prairie chicken conducts an elaborate dance to attract females for breeding. His ancient ritual can be observed from a blind or from your vehicle in a viewing area at the Comanche National Grassland, located near Campo, Colorado.

This courtship display can be seen from early March through mid-May. Arrive before daylight, be quiet, and never walk onto the birds' dancing grounds, known as leks. The best time to see the display is between sunrise and 9 A.M.—and you must remain in your vehicle, since prairie chickens are easily disturbed. If you plan on photographing from a blind, arrive one hour before daylight. Regulations say you must remain in the blind until at least one hour after sunrise. Contact the USDA Forest Service, P.O. Box 127, Springfield, CO 81073; phone (719) 523-6591. Call or write for a brochure and map. Be sure to make lodging reservations and check local road conditions before you visit.

IT'S A JUNGLE OUT THERE

Much of my work involves research on public opinion on and attitudes toward natural resources. Agencies use this information to make better policy decisions; private companies use the information to develop marketing plans for their hunting, fishing, and wildlife viewing products. My staff conducts telephone and mail surveys, and personal interviews. Talking to people at times can be, er, . . . enlightening.

Once we were completing a telephone survey of attitudes toward animals when one of my interviewers read the standard introduction to a respondent. It went something like, "Hello, my name is Dianne and I'm calling from Responsive Management and we are conducting a short survey for the Illinois Department of Conservation on the use of animals . . ."

"On what?" came the reply from an elderly woman.

"The use of animals," said the interviewer.

"The WHAT?" said the woman again.

"The use of animals," replied the interviewer, now preparing for a very long interview.

"The use of ENEMAS?" came the response. "Why do you want to talk to me about the use of enemas?"

Another survey we conducted was on public attitudes toward the Florida panther, one of the most endangered mammals in the United States. Several interviewers told me that the following exchange occurred more than once:

"Hello, my name is Chris, and I'm calling from Responsive Management to ask about your opinions on the Florida panther."

Following a pause, the individual would reply, "Oh, I'd like to answer your survey but I'm not interested in hockey."

It didn't take us long to figure out that the professional hockey team in Florida is . . . you guessed it . . . the Florida Panthers.

In another survey, one of the issues was whether or not the public supported having an agency manage deer for trophy ➤

➤ hunting. One gentleman never fully understood this question, and probably is still wondering why the state of Georgia is buying trophies for hunters.

Finally, not everyone answers our surveys. In another telephone survey we were conducting, a conversation went something like this:

"Hello, my name is David, and I'm calling on behalf of the department of natural resources, and we would like to ask you some questions on outdoor recreation."

"Sir, we don't go outside," the respondent answered, and hung up.

6 | Capturing
the Moment:
Wildlife photography

Many wildlife viewers are interested in photographing wildlife in the field. There are ways to get great photographic results without placing wildlife—or yourself—in jeopardy.

Vary Film Speeds

For best results with general wildlife photography, use medium-speed slide films such as ASA (ISO) 100 (Fujichrome or Ektachrome) or ASA 64 Kodachrome. For print film, use ASA 100 or 200. For landscape and scenic shots, use a slower-speed film such as Kodachrome 25, Velvia Fujichrome ASA 50, or Ektachrome 50 HC. Kodak's Ektar ASA 25 print film is excellent for enlargements.

Many photographers use film with an ASA of 100 or lower (known as "slow" film) because it enhances fine detail and won't appear grainy if enlarged. Slow film requires bright sunlight or a longer exposure time. For photographs in the early evening or early morning, use a faster film, rated ASA 250 or higher. Fast film is also better for moving animals, such as birds on the wing.

Early morning and late afternoon are the best times to photograph wildlife, for two reasons: wildlife is more apt to be active, and the quality of light at that time makes a better picture than the harsh light of midday.

Use the Right Lenses

Use a wide-angle lens (20 to 28 mm) to capture scenic shots. Use the greatest depth of field possible. Use a telephoto lens (200 to 400 mm) for the best close-up wildlife shots. Allowing space between the animals and the camera captures them more naturally and places them in their habitat.

A lens hood can help cut glare. It may also help protect the camera lens in the event it is bumped against another object.

Other Ideas

To produce sharp pictures, use a tripod. If shooting in dim light (early morning or late evening), consider using a shutter cable release. This will allow you to use a higher f-stop, which affords greater depth of field.

Take time to compose the shot.

Film and cameras should not be left in a closed vehicle during hot weather.

Stephen and Michele Vaughan, freelance writers and photographers from Colorado Springs, Colorado, contend, "The best equipment will not produce an outstanding image without an understanding of your subject. To become a good nature photographer, you must first become a good naturalist. The best way to learn about birds is to leave the camera bags behind, step into [the birds'] world and observe them. Educate yourself on where to find different species and how close to approach without spooking them."

The Reality Behind the Photograph

Laury Marshall, outdoor ethics director for the Izaak Walton League of America, points out the importance of understanding "the reality behind the photograph." Marshall remarks that many spectacular close-up shots of wildlife in books and magazines really weren't taken close-up, but were captured with a telephoto lens from a distance. Some of them show animals in a captive animal facility. She maintains that in many of the photographs appearing in magazines and books, the photographers appear to have been much closer than they actually were, giving a false impression to beginning wildlife photographers.

Chuck Bartlebaugh of the Center for Wildlife Information conveys how professional photographers get great photos:

■ They use captive and conditioned animals at game farms.

■ They photograph in controlled areas like Churchill (Canada) for polar bears, or the McNeil River Bear Sanctuary (Alaska) for grizzlies.

■ They use powerful telephoto lenses.

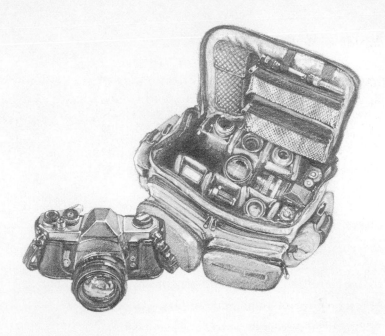

■ They are patient, devoting many years to getting desired photos in responsible ways.

Bartlebaugh notes, "Purchasing a camera does not give anyone permission to put animals, birds or marine life under stress."

"Another way professional photographers get great pictures is to shoot one heck of a lot of film," states Mark Hilliard, Watchable Wildlife Coordinator for the Bureau of Land Management. "If you only get one great picture out of a thousand, you've still got to shoot the thousand because you don't know whether the great photo will be the first shot, last shot, or one in between."

Safety Tips

Safety is a concern for wildlife photographers. As staff at Yellowstone National Park explained, "Photographers have been injured, and, on occasion, innocent bystanders [who were themselves maintaining a proper distance from the animals] were injured when the photographer caused the animal to charge."

Montana forester and photographer Bill Gabriel describes two gruesome episodes: "Two serious photographers with large telephoto lenses were killed by grizzly bears in Yellowstone and Glacier National Parks. . . . In the Glacier incident, film recovered from the camera of [the photographer] shows nearly forty photos of bears taken at various distances that indicated the bears had tried to move away, and he had followed them." In both episodes, the bear was a grizzly sow protecting her cubs.

Chuck Bartlebaugh offers the following guidelines for wildlife photographers who want to stay safe—and alive:

■ Photograph all animals from a vehicle or observation area, or at a distance with a 400 mm lens.

■ Remain alert to potential dangers despite your eagerness to take the perfect photo; maintain the recommended distance of five hundred to one thousand feet to avoid provoking large animals.

■ Never surprise an animal.

■ Retreat at any sign of stress or aggression.

■ Don't crouch or take a stance that may appear aggressive to a wild animal. Avoid following or chasing it; the animal may turn and charge.

■ Never surround an animal, crowd in on it, or try to herd it to a different location.

■ Never make unnecessary sounds to grab the animal's attention.

■ Stay out of dense brush. Avoid occupied dens and nests.

■ Be aware of other people in the area. Are their actions putting you in danger?

In nature photography there is one hard-and-fast rule of which the photographer must at all times observe the spirit: The welfare of the subject is more important than the photograph. This is not to say that photography should not be undertaken because of a slight risk to a common species. But the amount of risk which is acceptable decreases with the scarceness of the species, and the photographer should always do his utmost to minimize it.

"The Nature Photographer's Code of Practices"
by the Association of Natural History Photographic Societies

7 | Wildlife
for the
Future

Although every public opinion survey ever conducted on the subject shows that North Americans care deeply about wildlife and want to conserve and protect it, my research over the past decade has shown that very few people actually do anything to help wildlife. A citizenry that is concerned but does not act does not contribute to wildlife protection. Action counts.

People don't act on behalf of wildlife for several reasons. Sometimes people feel their efforts are futile. Some think that one

person can't make a difference. Others are too busy. One of the main reasons is that people don't really know what kinds of things they can do to help.

But believe this: Your efforts on behalf of wildlife are not futile. Little things can make a difference. Here are some big ways you can help assure wildlife's future:

Take a child birding, wildlife identifying, bug collecting, or wildlife photographing. Adult attitudes toward wildlife and the natural world are greatly influenced by childhood experiences. Nothing seems to foster positive attitudes toward wildlife more solidly than direct participation in wildlife-related activities at an early age.

Introduce a friend to wildlife viewing and birding. Research indicates there is an important link between birders (who actively identify species) and wildlife knowledge. In a national study on public attitudes toward wildlife, Dr. Stephen Kellert of Yale University concluded that the wildlife knowledge scores of committed birders were the highest of any demographic group examined in the entire study. The results suggested that active birding promotes an enhanced understanding of, awareness of, and concern for wildlife and the natural environment.

Buy yourself or a friend a copy of Aldo Leopold's *A Sand County Almanac*. Aldo Leopold is considered the father of wildlife management in America. His book *A Sand County Almanac*, written in the 1940s, is still the best book on wildlife ever written. By reading it, you will receive lessons on conservation, wildlife management, and ecology; the essays within it are written from the heart. Reading this book will give you a sense of our rich natural world.

Keep current on important wildlife issues facing your state or the nation. Check your local newspapers for information about current environmental issues. Read periodicals published by conservation groups. Here are a few worth checking out:

■ The National Wildlife Federation's *National Wildlife;* phone (703) 790-4000.

■ Defenders of Wildlife's *Defenders;* phone (202) 682-9400.

■ The National Audubon Society's *Audubon* or *Audubon Activist;* phone (212) 979-3000.

■ Izaak Walton League's *Outdoor Ethics Newsletter;* phone (301) 548-0150.

In addition, most state fish and wildlife agencies have magazines; nongame wildlife programs often publish newsletters. Check with your state fish and wildlife agency for availability.

Many other sources of information are available. Read as much as you can. Educate yourself, draw your own conclusions, and proceed accordingly. Only by getting into details can you support the right thing.

Write a letter. One of the most important actions a citizen can take also happens to be one of the easiest—writing letters. Letters to elected officials, such as your representative or senator, and letters to federal and state wildlife and environmental agencies can make a big difference. Your opinion counts. When officials receive enough letters about an issue, they do take notice.

Dan Witter of the Missouri Department of Conservation once told me about a conversation he'd had with a congressman. The congressman explained that he was surprised that a certain issue was such a hot topic and that so many people supported wildlife. Dan was surprised, too. "How many letters did you receive?" asked Dan. "Seven" was the reply.

Seven! Your opinion counts!

Most citizens think writing letters is a waste of time, and don't take advantage of this important wildlife conservation tool. The result? Public officials often don't know what people think about issues, and when they don't hear anything, they assume the public doesn't care.

Letters to elected officials in Washington helped pass important legislation for wildlife such as the Endangered Species Act, the Clean Water Act, and the Alaskan Lands Protection Act, which preserved millions of acres of land for wildlife. The National Wildlife Federation advises that the best time to write a letter to a legislator is before he or she must vote on a bill. The best time to write a letter to an environmental or wildlife agency is when a regulation has been proposed but not yet approved.

Be concise when you write. The National Wildlife Federation advises that you stick to one issue and use your own words—don't parrot something someone else has told you to say. Explain why you feel the way you do. It doesn't have to be technical, but explain how the issue affects you. Most importantly, ask the legislator or agency to do something specific: pass a regulation, vote for a particular bill, request hearings, or cosponsor a bill.

The letter needn't be typed, but write legibly. Ask for a reply.

You can contact a member of the U.S. House of Representatives by writing: The Honorable _____, U.S. House of Representatives, Washington, DC 20515. You can contact a U.S. Senator by writing: The Honorable_____, U.S. Senate, Washington, DC 20510. If you don't know the names of your senators or representatives, call your local library and ask them to find out for you. Give them the number of your voting district from your voter registration card, or tell them where you live, so they'll be able to identify your particular legislator.

Telephone your legislator. Telephone calls effectively relay last-minute messages to your state capitol or Washington, D.C. When you call, be polite and specific. Express your opinion, but also say what you want the legislator to do—vote for a particular issue, etc. Legislators keep tabs on their phone calls and tally calls and letters to gauge public opinion.

To reach your U.S. Senator or Representative by phone, call the Capitol switchboard at (202) 224-3121. The operator can furnish you with a needed number or connect you directly. To reach local legislators and officials, call your state government switchboard.

Write a letter to the editor of your newspaper. You'd be surprised how many opinion leaders, city officials, and citizens read the letters-to-the-editor section in newspapers. Elected officials often scan letters in local papers to assess public opinion. Before you write, get your facts straight and express your thoughts clearly. Be reasonable and avoid being preachy, and you will have a better chance of being published. Urge others to join you in doing something about the issue.

Meet with your legislator. Legislators meet with their constituents to stay in touch with their electors. Legislators need citizen support— that's how they get into office. Why not meet with your elected official about a wildlife issue and make your opinions known?

Report wildlife violators. If you know or even suspect that a wildlife law is being broken, report it to your state fish and wildlife agency. Most state agencies have toll-free numbers for reporting offenses, so the call won't cost anything. If you choose, you may remain anonymous and will not be required to appear in court. You may even get a reward if your report leads to an arrest. More importantly, you will have the satisfaction of knowing you have assisted wildlife law enforcement officers in catching poachers and others who abuse wildlife and wild habitats.

Donate to your state fish and wildlife agency's nongame wildlife program. Most state fish and wildlife agencies have a nongame wildlife program. Unlike a sportsman's program, this program manages wildlife areas for nonhunted species such as hawks, owls, frogs, and turtles. Many of these programs rely on donations to fund their conservation efforts. In many states, you can check off a box on your state income tax forms to donate to this cause as you file your state income tax.

Inquire about how your state funds its nongame wildlife program and share this knowledge with others. If you have an accountant prepare your taxes, tell him you would like to check the appropriate box and donate to the program.

Purchase a Migratory Bird Hunting Stamp (Duck Stamp) each year.
Proceeds from the sale of Duck Stamps purchase wetlands as wildlife refuges. Duck Stamp revenue goes directly to the acquisition of such land. Since 1934, the Duck Stamp program has conserved nearly four million acres of wetlands and other habitat. Duck stamps are sold at most post offices and most national wildlife refuges.

Landscape with native vegetation. Plant native vegetation around your home to attract wildlife, conserve water, and minimize fertilizer and pesticide use. Contact a local greenhouse or nursery to find sources for native plants. Your state fish and wildlife agency's nongame wildlife program or cooperative extension office can offer tips on getting started.

Volunteer for wildlife. Many state fish and wildlife agencies and private conservation groups rely on volunteers. You can volunteer to be an observer in the National Audubon Society's Christmas Bird Count. Each Christmas, more than 43,000 volunteers from all fifty states, every Canadian province, and territories and nations in the Caribbean, Central America, South America, and the Pacific count every bird and bird species seen during a twenty-four-hour period (from midnight to midnight). The entire count takes place during a two-and-a-half-week period beginning in mid-December. The Christmas Bird Count provides important trend data on bird populations. To participate, call the National Audubon Society at 700 Broadway, New York, NY 10003-9501; phone (212) 979-3083.

Save a snag. Many of America's cavity-nesting bird populations are declining. Eastern bluebirds, brown-headed nuthatches, red-headed woodpeckers, and northern flickers share one major reason for their decline: the loss of snags that provide foraging and cavities for nesting. Where safe and practical, let dead trees stand, and encourage your neighbors and others to do the same.

Build a nest box. Artificial nest boxes can enhance local cavity-nesting bird populations. There's an especially high demand for nest boxes to accommodate American kestrels and bluebirds. For instructions on how to build nest boxes, contact your state fish and wildlife agency. For information on how to build a bluebird nest box, contact the North American Bluebird Society, P.O. Box 6295, Silver Spring, MD 20906; phone (301) 384-2798.

Don't pick up "orphaned" animals. If you find an animal "left" alongside a road or in a field, it's probably not abandoned. The best thing you can do is leave it where it is. Its mother is more than likely watching from nearby, waiting for you to go.

Don't abandon a pet in the wild. Abandoned animals severely impact native wildlife, often killing wild animals in order to survive. Domestic cats can wreak havoc on backyard birds. Consider declawing your kitten/cat and keeping it inside. And don't dump those fish from your aquarium into natural waters; many species of fish can and have established themselves in North American lakes and streams, wreaking havoc on native fish populations.

Learn about pets before you buy them. Sometimes our love for animals can adversely affect wild populations. Some South American parrot populations have declined because of public demand for them as pets. When choosing a pet, pick captive-bred animals over wild ones. Learn if the pet of your dreams should stay where it naturally lives. Learn all you can about an animal and whether the pet trade affects its status in the wild. If it does, choose another species. For more information, contact TRAFFIC USA, World Wildlife Fund, 1250 24th Street NW, Washington, DC 20037; phone (202) 293-4800.

Don't buy animal products made from endangered species. Despite national and international laws regulating trade in endangered species, illegal imports still make their way to North America. Avoid purchasing ivory, buying products made from certain reptiles, and collecting corals; these activities may be bringing some forms of wildlife to the brink of extinction. For more information, contact TRAFFIC USA [see above].

Get a friend to join and support a conservation organization. The bright, energetic, and devoted staffs of North America's wildlife and conservation organizations count on you for support. If you don't belong to such an organization, join one. If you belong to one, join another. Get a friend to join, too. By doing so you not only support the organization financially, assisting its wildlife endeavors, but you also add important political clout. Politicians often judge organizations by the size of their membership. Imagine the president of the National Wildlife Federation being able to say, "I represent more than ten thousand members/supporters." Now imagine that president saying, "I represent four million Americans."

More than one thousand organizations actively work to protect North America's wildlife and environment. For a listing of these groups and their addresses, purchase the National Wildlife Federation's Conservation Directory by calling (800) 432-6564; ask for item #79561.

TAKING ACTION

Several years ago, while working for a state fish and wildlife agency, I had the opportunity to evaluate my agency's wildlife education efforts. After a review, I saw clearly that the common theme we were sending citizens was that they should be concerned about wildlife. But after conducting several public opinion polls and a series of focus groups, I was forced to the conclusion that citizens were already concerned. What they weren't doing was acting on behalf of wildlife, and we weren't teaching them how.

My research indicated that citizens did not know specific things they could do. I concluded that the agency needed to publicize the ways people could help wildlife. I immediately went to work writing an article entitled, "Fifty Ways a Citizen Can Help Conserve Wildlife." After finishing the piece, I had to face a difficult fact: my article had to go through a lengthy agency review before it could be approved for publication. Since all of my previous articles and reports had been approved, I had an idea: I would submit the article for review while at the same time submitting the article to a magazine. I knew it would take several months for the article to hit the newsstands, and the agency review would take several months as well. I thought I would simply reduce by half the time it would take for my crucial message to reach the citizenry.

Imagine my excitement when the magazine editor called to say she loved the article and would publish it. Imagine my surprise when, the very next day, a rather perturbed division director stormed into my office and proceeded to reprimand me, saying it was inappropriate for a public employee to write an article on environmental action. The article would not be approved for publication.

➤

> But . . . but . . . but . . .

I admitted that I had (somewhat hastily) submitted the article and that it would be published that month. The response was clear: publish the article and you might be looking for a new job. The editor wasn't happy when I asked that she pull the piece.

Bureaucracy did serve some purpose after all. After several discussions with the editor and the division director, we reached a compromise: the editor would publish the article without reference to my status as a public employee and get rid of a few of the more nocuous "ways a citizen can help wildlife." The article was eventually published with the title, "Twenty-Three Ways a Citizen Can Help Conserve Wildlife." The title didn't have the same ring as it had at the start. But I still had a job.

111

EPILOGUE

I wrote this book to help you get started watching wildlife. I intended to help you begin a lifelong pursuit of watching wild animals. I wanted to write a how-to guide but keep it simple and focused. In doing so, I was forced to exclude an enormous amount of detailed information, some of which you can find in field guides, magazines, books, and governmental literature. This book is only a beginning.

Throughout these pages, I've used larger, more glamorous species as examples of wildlife watching and its thrills. But we can observe all animals, and many times the best wildlife watching opportunities involve common species, many from our own backyards. If anything in this book compels you to notice something about wild animals, near or far, that you have never noticed before, I will have accomplished what I set out to do.

You will find that the more you learn about wildlife, the more you realize there is to learn. You will also find yourself perceiving more and more about our natural world; the seasons, different habitats, the numerous species that live around you. Many of these perceptions can never be adequately captured with words. Perhaps Aldo Leopold said it best when he wrote, "Our ability to perceive quality in nature begins, as in art, with the pretty. It expands through successive stages of the beautiful to values yet uncaptured by language. The quality of cranes lies, I think, in this higher gamut, as yet beyond the reach of words."

I write because I believe that North America's wildlife exists in delicate balance. We have destroyed wildlife and, in some cases, we have restored it. Bald eagles were in serious decline two decades ago because of human actions, but they now appear to be on their way to recovery because of human efforts. Having inherited a rich and glorious world from our ancestors, we now have the critical responsibility to safeguard it for our children and grandchildren. Theodore Roosevelt, one of America's eminent conservationists, phrased it best when he said, "Wild beasts and birds are by right not the property merely of the people alive today, but the property of unborn generations, whose belongings we have no right to squander."

113

LIST OF ILLUSTRATIONS

ABOUT THE AUTHOR

Wildlife biologist Mark Damian Duda has traveled extensively, from the Everglades in south Florida to Denali National Park in Alaska, to watch and photograph wildlife. His first-hand experiences watching orcas off the coast of British Columbia, grizzly bears in Alaska, bighorn sheep in Colorado, black bears in Tennessee, snow geese in Virginia, and humpback whales off the coast of California have instilled in him a strong desire to teach others how to view wildlife successfully and ethically.

Mark is the executive director of Responsive Management, an international natural resource consulting firm that assists natural resource, environmental, and outdoor recreation organizations, helping them to better understand their customers and constituents. He has worked as a consultant to more than forty state fish and wildlife agencies, and for the U.S. Fish and Wildlife Service, the Canadian Wildlife Service, USDA Forest Service, Bureau of Land Management, International Association of Fish and Wildlife Agencies, and many private conservation groups, including the Izaak Walton League of America, Wildlife Management Institute, and the American Sportfishing Association.

Mark is a noted authority on wildlife viewing, and a regular speaker at Watchable Wildlife Program conferences. He has been instrumental in initiating and developing wildlife viewing programs and enthusiasm nationwide. Author of more than fifty papers, book chapters, journal articles, and scientific reports on wildlife viewing and conservation, he is also the author of the *Virginia Wildlife Viewing Guide*.

Mark was named Conservation Educator of the Year by the Florida Wildlife Federation and the National Wildlife Federation and was the recipient of the Western Association of Fish and Wildlife Agencies 1995 Special Conservation Achievement Award. He holds a master's degree from Yale University in natural resource policy and planning and is a native Virginian living in the Shenandoah Valley. He can be reached at Responsive Management, P.O. Box 389, Harrisonburg, VA 22801.

FALCON GUIDES

THE WATCHABLE WILDLIFE SERIES
Arizona Wildlife Viewing Guide
California Wildlife Viewing Guide
Colorado Wildlife Viewing Guide
Florida Wildlife Viewing Guide
Idaho Wildlife Viewing Guide
Indiana Wildlife Viewing Guide
Iowa Wildlife Viewing Guide
Kentucky Wildlife Viewing Guide
Montana Wildlife Viewing Guide
Nevada Wildlife Viewing Guide
New Mexico Wildlife Viewing Guide
North Carolina Wildlife Viewing Guide
North Dakota Wildlife Viewing Guide
Oregon Wildlife Viewing Guide
Tennessee Wildlife Viewing Guide
Texas Wildlife Viewing Guide
Utah Wildlife Viewing Guide
Vermont Wildlife Viewing Guide
Virginia Wildlife Viewing Guide
Washington Wildlife Viewing Guide
Wisconsin Wildlife Viewing Guide

BIRDER'S GUIDES
Birding Arizona
Birder's Guide to Montana
Birding Minnesota

SCENIC DRIVING GUIDES
Scenic Byways
Scenic Byways II
Back Country Byways
Arizona Scenic Drives
California Scenic Drives
Colorado Scenic Drives
Montana Scenic Drives
New Mexico Scenic Drives
Oregon Scenic Drives
Scenic Driving Georgia
Texas Scenic Drives
Traveler's Guide to the Lewis & Clark Trail
Traveler's Guide to the Oregon Trail
Traveler's Guide to the Pony Express Trail

ROCKHOUND'S GUIDES
Rockhounding Arizona
Rockhound's Guide to California
Rockhound's Guide to Colorado
Rockhound's Guide to Montana
Rockhound's Guide to New Mexico
Rockhound's Guide to Texas

■ *To order any of these books, or to request an expanded list of available titles, including guides for viewing wildlife, birding, scenic driving, or rockhounding, please call 1-800-582-2665, or write to Falcon, PO Box 1718, Helena, MT 59624.*

take time to
learn more

With this **VIDEO**, a companion to the book, *Watching Wildlife*, you'll discover the best and latest techniques for viewing wildlife in natural surroundings. Take time to learn more and increase your chances of seeing wild animals on any outdoor excursion.

what you'll discover:

- Techniques for seeing animals without disturbing them.
- Where and when to go for the best viewing.
- Ideas for including children on wildlife viewing trips.
- How to identify tracks and other signs of wildlife activity.

Watching Wildlife Video
A Guide to One of America's Most Popular Activities
VHS, 30 minutes. $19.95

To order or to request a catalog,
please call 1-800-582-2665